JESUIT RELIGIOUS LIFE

TODAY

Series I. Jesuit Primary Sources, in English Translations

No. 1.   St. Ignatius of Loyola. *The Constitutions of the Society of Jesus. Translated, with an Introduction and a Commentary,* by George E. Ganss, S.J.

No. 2.   *Documents of the 31st and 32nd General Congregations of the Society of Jesus. An English Translation.* Prepared by the Jesuit Conference and edited by John W. Padberg, S.J.

No. 3.   *Jesuit Religious Life Today. The Principal Features of Its Spirit, in Excerpts from Papal Documents, St. Ignatius' Constitutions, the 31st and 32nd General Congregations, and Letters of Father General Pedro Arrupe.* Edited by George E. Ganss, S.J.

JESUIT RELIGIOUS LIFE TODAY

The Principal Features of Its Spirit,

in Excerpts from

Papal Documents,

St. Ignatius' *Constitutions*,

the 31st and 32nd General Congregations,

and Letters of Father General Pedro Arrupe

Edited by George E. Ganss, S.J.

THE INSTITUTE OF JESUIT SOURCES
St. Louis, 1977

All the excerpts in this book are translations of official documents, and were taken from the following publications of the Institute of Jesuit Sources, St. Louis, Missouri:
(1) Saint Ignatius of Loyola. *The Constitutions of the Society of Jesus. Translated, with an Introduction and a Commentary,* by George E. Ganss, S.J. 1970.
(2) *Documents of the 31st and 32nd General Congregations of the Society of Jesus.* Edited by John W. Padberg, S.J. 1977.
(3) *Jesuit Religious Life. A Summary of Orientations and Norms.* 1977.

IMPRIMI POTEST: Very Reverend Leo F. Weber, S.J.
                Provincial of the Missouri Province
                August 4, 1977

IMPRIMATUR   John J. Cardinal Carberry
                Archbishop of St. Louis
                August 19, 1977

Library of Congress Card Catalogue Number: 77-78816
ISBN 0-912422-27-0 paperback
ISBN 0-912422-29-7 Smyth sewn paperbound

CONTENTS

Part II Adaptation of the Charism (Continued)

Editor's Foreword

In its decree on the updated renewal of religious life (*Perfectae caritatis,* no. 2), Vatican Council II urged the members of religious institutes to a twofold task: (1) to study the spirit or charism of their founders and (2) to update their institutes by applying that spirit to the changed conditions of modern times. By this summons the Council unobtrusively changed a century-old trend of the Holy See in dealing with religious institutes. While they were slowly recovering throughout the nineteenth century from their near extinction during the period 1773 to about 1810, and while many new congregations especially of women were being founded, the Holy See tended to insist on directives which drew these institutes into greater and greater uniformity, especially in details unessential to religious life itself. This can be seen in the *Normae* of 1901 which much influenced the treatment of religious life in the Code of Canon Law issued in 1917.

Viewed against that background, the summons of Vatican II appears as an invitation to each institute to discover and be itself.[1] The Council states its reasons for its action: "It is for the good of the Church that institutes have their own proper characters and functions." These elements had usually been expressed in the spirit and aims of each founder, which were to "be faithfully accepted and retained." This task to which the Council calls religious, as a little reflection shows, has no end in the fairly near future. For religious life, like the Church herself, will always need updating. "Ecclesia semper reformanda."

---

1 On this topic see the chapter on "Religious" by R. A. Hill, S.J. in "The Pastoral Guide to Canon Law," *Chicago Studies,* XV (fall, 1976), esp. 316-319.

The present small book, *Jesuit Religious Life Today,* shows through excerpts from official documents the point which the Society of Jesus has reached after some twelve years of effort since 1965 to respond to the Council's summons.

Some origins of this book stem from far back. For over four centuries after St. Ignatius' death in 1556, Jesuits kept fresh in mind the chief features of their Institute by means of two sets of excerpts which they heard at table every month, the "Summary of the Constitutions" and the "Common Rules." In 1966, however, the 31st General Congregation found updating desirable for both these sets, as will be explained more fully below on pages 89-90 and 99-100.

Consequently Father General Pedro Arrupe issued to the whole Society two new booklets of excerpts, respectively successors to the two ancient sets: (1) *Sancti Patris Ignatii excerpta Constitutionum* of January 2, 1968, at the instigation of the 31st General Congregation and (2) *De vita religiosa in Societate Iesu* of December 31, 1975, at the instigation of the 32nd Congregation. The present small book grew gradually around these two booklets of Father Arrupe, first by their being planned to fit together between one cover and then, because of a suggestion from him, by their being placed within a framework of papal documents. Thus all three sets of excerpts give support to one another, somewhat like the warp, the woof, and the framework of a loom on which they are stretched.

The book falls naturally into two parts.

Part I, The Founder's Spirit, presents readings from the writings of St. Ignatius and his sixteenth-century associates, selected to show the spirit or tenor of thought which they projected into their Institute of the Society of Jesus.

Part II, Adaptation of the Founder's Charism to Modern Times, presents from official documents key passages which pertain to the work of adapting the ancient heritage to modern circumstances. These readings regard principally the areas of personal and communitarian religious life, rather than the apostolate or government (with which, however, they occasionally overlap). They reflect especially the decrees of the 31st General Congregation (1965-1966) and the 32nd General Congregation (1974-1975), but also the deliberations, conducted in Jesuit communities and committees throughout the world, which led up to those decrees.

These deliberations and other efforts in our era of change were carried on amid joys and sorrows, successes and failures, some experimental measures which will turn out to be permanent gains and some which may be found to need further modification or even abrogation. Hence this small book is made available to any who are interested, Jesuits and non-Jesuits, not in any triumphalistic spirit of achievement, but in a willingness to share our fortunes and misfortunes with our sisters and brothers, in the hope that they may glean from it some help and guidance as they too make their way along the sometimes difficult road of responding to the Council's call.

This book is intended especially to serve as a vademecum for reflection and prayer. In its present form it owes its origin and completion to suggestions and constant encouragement from Father General Pedro Arrupe, from his American Assistant Father Gerald R. Sheahan, and from the President and other members of the Jesuit Conference of Provincials in the United States. This editor expresses his heartfelt gratitude to them, and also to many others who have helped in a variety of ways.

> George E. Ganss, S.J.
> Director and General Editor
> The Institute of Jesuit Sources

Abbreviations Used in the Footnotes

AAS	*Acta Apostolicae Sedis*
ActRSJ	*Acta Romana Societatis Iesu*
CIC	*Codex Iuris Canonici*
CollDecr	*Collectio Decretorum Congregationum Generalium Societatis Iesu.* Rome, 1961.
Cons	The *Constitutions of the Society of Jesus*
*Cons*MHSJ	*Constitutiones Societatis Iesu* in the series of the Monumenta Historica Societatis Iesu. 4 volumes
D	Decree
DocsGC31and32	*Documents of the 31st and 32nd General Congregations of the Society of Jesus.* St. Louis, 1977.
Ep	*Epitome Instituti Societatis Iesu*
EppIgn	*Sti. Ignatii Epistolae.* 12 volumes
FI	Formula of the Institute
GC	General Congregation
GenExam	The *General Examen*
InstSJ	*Institutum Societatis Iesu.* 3 volumes. Florence, 1892-1893.
MHSJ	Monumenta Historica Societatis Iesu
SpEx	The *Spiritual Exercises* of St. Ignatius
Vat. II	Vatican Council II

PART I: THE FOUNDER'S SPIRIT

A. The Formula of the Institute
of Pope Julius III, 1550

Editor's Introduction

The fundamental Rule for the foundation and government of the Society of Jesus is the papally approved "Formula of the Institute" as contained first in the bull *Regimini militantis Ecclesiae* of September 27, 1540 and then, with small revisions, in the bull *Exposcit debitum* of July 21, 1550.

After St. Ignatius of Loyola and his first companions had vowed at Paris in 1534 to devote themselves totally to God in apostolic service, they prayerfully deliberated in the spring of 1539 whether or not they should bind themselves together in a new religious institute. They unanimously reached an affirmative conclusion. They outlined the chief features of their proposed congregation in a document of some seven pages entitled "First Sketch of the Institute of the Society of Jesus," which they submitted in June or July to Pope Paul III. It is probable that Ignatius himself wrote this document in Spanish and that someone else among his companions, possibly Codure or Salmerón, translated it into polished Latin. In any case, the founder greatly influenced the composition, for the "First Sketch" unmistakably reflects the personal outlook on spiritual and apostolic life which Ignatius communicated to his first companions.

Pope Paul approved this document verbally in September, 1539. After small changes, chiefly stylistic, made by his canonists, he incorporated the sketch into his bull *Regimini militantis Ecclesiae* by which he officially approved the foundation of the Society of Jesus on September 27, 1540. Ten years of experience suggested a few additions or slight changes, which Pope Julius III incorporated into a new bull of July 21, 1550, *Exposcit debitum.*

This Formula of the Institute as contained in the bull of 1550 is the papal Rule still in force today. Since it is the fundamental law of the Society of Jesus, it is often printed as a kind of preface in modern editions of Ignatius' *Constitutions.* Hence the chief passages from it have a fitting place among the excerpts from papal documents contained in the present book.

READINGS FROM

THE FORMULA OF THE INSTITUTE

as found in the bull *Exposcit debitum*
of Pope Julius III, July 21, 1550

[2]. Now . . . a petition has been humbly submitted to us. It begs us to confirm the formula which now contains the aforementioned Society's Institute, expressed more accurately and clearly than before [by our predecessor, Pope Paul III, in 1540], because of the lessons learned through experience and usage, but in the same spirit. The content of that formula follows, and it is this:

[3]. [1].[1] Whoever desires to serve as a soldier of God beneath the banner of the cross in our Society, which we desire to be designated by the name of Jesus, and to serve the Lord alone and the Church, His spouse, under the Roman pontiff, the vicar of Christ on earth, should, after a solemn vow of perpetual chastity, poverty, and obedience, keep what follows in mind. He is a member of a Society founded chiefly for this purpose: to strive especially for the

---

1 Different editors of the bull *Exposcit debitum* have variously divided it into sections and numbered them differently. Consequently passages sought because of references in different books cannot be readily found in a modern edition of the bull unless it presents both systems of numbering, as is done here. The bold face numbers in square brackets are from *Cons*MHSJ, I; those in light face type are from *Epitome Instituti Societatis Iesu*.

defense and propagation of the faith and for the progress of souls in Christian life and doctrine, by means of public preaching, lectures, and any other ministration whatsoever of the word of God, and further by means of the Spiritual Exercises, the education of children and unlettered persons in Christianity, and the spiritual consolation of Christ's faithful through hearing confessions and administering the other sacraments. Moreover, this Society should show itself no less useful in reconciling the estranged, in holily assisting and serving those who are found in prisons or hospitals, and indeed in performing any other works of charity, according to what will seem expedient for the glory of God and the common good. Furthermore, all these works should be carried out altogether free of charge and without accepting any salary for the labor expended in all the aforementioned activities. Still further, let any such person take care, as long as he lives, first of all to keep before his eyes God and then the nature of this Institute which he has embraced and which is, so to speak, a pathway to God; and then let him strive with all his effort to achieve this end set before him by God—each one, however, according to the grace which the Holy Spirit has given to him and according to the particular grade of his own vocation.

[2]. Consequently, lest anyone should perhaps show zeal, but a zeal which is not according to knowledge, the decision about each one's grade and the selection and entire distribution of employments shall be in the power of the superior general or ordinary who at any future time is to be elected by us, or in the power of those whom this superior general may appoint under himself with that authority, in order that the proper order necessary in every well-organized community may be preserved. This superior general, with the advice of his associates, shall possess the authority to establish constitutions leading to the achievement of this end which has been proposed to us, with the majority of votes always having the right to prevail. He shall also have the authority to explain officially doubts which may arise in connection with our Institute as comprised within this For-

mula. The council,[2] which must necessarily be convoked to establish or change the Constitutions and for other matters of more than ordinary importance, such as the alienation or dissolution of houses and colleges once erected, should be understood (according to the explanation in our Constitutions) to be the greater part of the entire professed Society which can be summoned without grave inconvenience by the superior general. In other matters, which are of lesser importance, the same general, aided by counsel from his brethren to the extent that he will deem fitting, shall have the full right personally to order and command whatever he judges in the Lord to pertain to the glory of God and the common good, as will be explained in the Constitutions.

[4]. [3]. All who make the profession in this Society should understand at the time, and furthermore keep in mind as long as they live, that this entire Society and the individual members who make their profession in it are campaigning for God under faithful obedience to His Holiness Pope Paul III and his successors in the Roman pontificate. The Gospel does indeed teach us, and we know from the orthodox faith and firmly hold, that all of Christ's faithful are subject to the Roman pontiff as their head and as the vicar of Jesus Christ. But we have judged nevertheless that the following procedure will be supremely profitable to each of us and to any others who will pronounce the same profession in the future, for the sake of our greater devotion in obedience to the Apostolic See, of greater abnegation of our own wills, and of surer direction from the Holy Spirit. In addition to that ordinary bond of the three vows, we are to be obliged by a special vow to carry out whatever the present and future Roman pontiffs may order which pertains to the progress of souls and the propagation of the faith; and to go without subterfuge or excuse, as far as in us lies, to whatsoever provinces they may choose to send us—whether they

---

2 This "council" was later termed a "general congregation," in *Cons*, [677, 682, 687], or a "general chapter" in [441, 655, 681].

are pleased to send us among the Turks or any other infidels, even those who live in the region called the Indies, or among any heretics whatever, or schismatics, or any of the faithful.

[4]. Therefore before those who will come to us take this burden upon their shoulders, they should ponder long and seriously, as the Lord has counseled [Luke 14:30], whether they possess among their resources enough spiritual capital to complete this tower; that is, whether the Holy Spirit who moves them is offering them so much grace that with His aid they have hope of bearing the weight of this vocation. Then, after they have enlisted through the inspiration of the Lord in this militia of Christ, they ought to be prompt in carrying out this obligation which is so great, being clad for battle day and night [Eph. 6:14; 1 Peter 1:13].

[5]. However, to forestall among us any ambition of such missions or provinces, or any refusal of them, all our members should have this understanding: They should not either directly or through someone else carry on negotiations with the Roman pontiff about such missions, but leave all this care to God, and to the pope himself as God's vicar, and to the superior general of the Society. This general too, just like the rest, should not treat with the said pontiff about his being sent to one region or another, unless after advice from the Society.

[6]. All should likewise vow that in all matters which promote the observance of this Rule they will be obedient to the one put in charge of the Society. (He should be as qualified as possible for this office and will be elected by a majority of the votes, as will be explained in the Constitutions.) Moreover, he should possess all the authority and power over the Society which are useful for its good administration, correction, and government. He should issue the commands which he knows to be opportune for achieving the end set before him by God and the Society. In his superiorship he should be ever mindful of the kindness, meekness, and charity of Christ and of the pattern

set by Peter and Paul,[3] a norm which both he and the aforementioned council should keep constantly in view. Assuredly, too, because of the great utility to the order and for the sake of the constant practice of humility which has never been sufficiently praised, the individual subjects should not only be obliged to obey the general in all matters pertaining to the Society's Institute but also to recognize and properly venerate Christ as present in him.

[**5**]. [7]. From experience we have learned that a life removed as far as possible from all infection of avarice and as like as possible to evangelical poverty is more gratifying, more undefiled, and more suitable for the edification of our fellowmen. We likewise know that our Lord Jesus Christ will supply to His servants who are seeking only the kingdom of God what is necessary for food and clothing. Therefore our members, one and all, should vow perpetual poverty in such a manner that neither the professed, either as individuals or in common, nor any house or church of theirs can acquire any civil right to any produce, fixed revenues, or possessions or to the retention of any stable goods (except those which are proper for their own use and habitation); but they should instead be content with whatever is given them out of charity for the necessities of life.

[8]. However, the houses which the Lord will provide are to be dedicated to labor in His vineyard and not to the pursuit of scholastic studies; and on the other hand, it appears altogether proper that workers should be provided for that same vineyard from among the young men who are inclined to piety and capable of applying themselves to learning, in order that they may form a kind of seminary for the Society, including the professed Society. Consequently, to provide facilities for studies, the professed Society should be capable

---

3 The "pattern set by Peter and Paul" can be found in 1 Peter 5:1-3; Phil. 3:17; 2 Thess. 3:7-9; 1 Tim. 4:12; and Titus 1:7.

of possessing colleges of scholastics wherever benefactors will be moved by their devotion to build and endow them. We now petition that as soon as these colleges will have been built and endowed (but not from resources which it pertains to the Holy See to apply), they may be established through authorization from the Holy See or considered to be so established. These colleges should be capable of possessing fixed revenues, rights to rentals, or possessions which are to be applied to the uses and needs of the students. The general or the Society retains the full government or superintendency over the aforementioned colleges and students; and this pertains to the choice of the rectors or governors and of the scholastics; the admission, dismissal, reception, and exclusion of the same; the enactment of statutes; the arrangement, instruction, edification, and correction of the scholastics; the manner of supplying them with food, clothing, and all the other necessary materials; and every other kind of government, control, and care. All this should be managed in such a way that neither may the students be able to abuse the aforementioned goods nor may the professed Society be able to convert them to its own uses, but may use them to provide for the needs of the scholastics. These students, moreover, should have such intellectual ability and moral character as to give solid hope that they will be suitable for the Society's functions after their studies are completed, and that thus at length, after their progress in spirit and learning has become manifest and after sufficient testing, they can be admitted into our Society.

[6]. Since all the members should be priests, they should be obliged to recite the Divine Office according to the ordinary rite of the Church, but privately and not in common or in choir. Also, in what pertains to food, clothing, and other external things, they will follow the common and approved usage of reputable priests, so that if anything is subtracted in this regard in accordance with each one's need or desire of spiritual progress, it may be offered, as will be fitting, out of devotion and not obligation, as a reasonable service of the body to God.

[9]. These are the matters which we were able to explain about our profession in a kind of sketch, through the good pleasure of our previously mentioned sovereign pontiff Paul and of the Apostolic See. We have now completed this explanation, in order to give brief information both to those who ask us about our plan of life and also to those who will later follow us if, God willing, we shall ever have imitators along this path. By experience we have learned that the path has many and great difficulties connected with it. Consequently we have judged it opportune to decree that no one should be permitted to pronounce his profession in this Society unless his life and doctrine have been probed by long and exacting tests (as will be explained in the Constitutions). For in all truth this Institute requires men who are thoroughly humble and prudent in Christ as well as conspicuous in the integrity of Christian life and learning. Moreover, some persons will be admitted to become coadjutors either for spiritual or temporal concerns or to become scholastics. After sufficient probations and the time specified in the Constitutions, these too should, for their greater devotion and merit, pronounce their vows. But their vows will not be solemn (except in the case of some who with permission from the superior general will be able to make three solemn vows of this kind because of their devotion and personal worth). Instead, they will be vows by which these persons are bound as long as the superior general thinks that they should be retained in the Society, as will be explained more fully in the Constitutions. But these coadjutors and scholastics too should be admitted into this militia of Jesus Christ only after they have been diligently examined and found suitable for that same end of the Society. And may Christ deign to be favorable to these our tender beginnings, to the glory of God the Father, to whom alone be glory and honor forever. Amen.

[7]. Wherefore we . . . , by our apostolic authority . . . forever approve and confirm the founding and organizing of the Society, and the extension of that number of its members, of the acceptance and admission of coadjutors,

and its privileges one and all, immunities, exemptions, and liberties both to establish and alter statutes and ordinances, and any other indults which our predecessor and this Apostolic See thereby granted to the Society and its general.

PART I: THE FOUNDER'S SPIRIT
(continued)

B. The *Constitutions of the Society of Jesus*
by St. Ignatius of Loyola

PREFACE BY FATHER PEDRO ARRUPE

The *Constitutions,* which St. Ignatius composed so carefully and bequeathed to the Society he founded, remain for all Jesuits the pure font from which to draw the spirit of their vocation. The complete text of the *Constitutions* ought to be read and pondered, over and over again, both in private and in community gatherings. For in them, as the preface to the first edition of the *Constitutions* in 1559 states, "are contained the sinews of our Society, the firm foundation of its religious institute, and those bonds by which its whole body should be tied and held together."

To make the way to a deep personal and interior knowledge of these *Constitutions* easier, I have deemed it opportune to select from them and publish some excerpts, extensive enough to avoid omission of any point essential to the spiritual progress of all of us, yet also brief enough for them to be read and reread often. They do not in any way substitute for the complete text, which all Jesuits ought to consult with diligence. Rather, they are meant to make up a small manual which, wherever we are, we shall have ready at hand. In this way it will help us, I hope, to keep the principal themes of the *Constitutions* fresh in memory and engraved on our hearts.

The selection of such excerpts, as everyone knows, is anything but free from difficulties. One must take account of three elements: the doctrine, which, objectively considered, scarcely admits abbreviation; the genuine meaning or importance, which each paragraph derives from its context; and the preservation of proper proportion in the subject-matters chosen. These excerpts, therefore, ought not to be

15

regarded as comprehensive expositions of their respective topics, nor as a kind of résumé of the Society's juridical norms. Rather, their aim is to aid our members toward frequent spiritual reading and prayer.

The manual follows the division of the *Constitutions* into ten parts. The text of the paragraphs, as transcribed, is not altered, except in some minor details necessary for the editing. The excerpts from the *General Examen* are taken only from chapter four. The *Examen* is indeed addressed to candidates, but its principles retain their force throughout the life of all. Chapter four throws clear light on the manner of our identification with Christ, in accordance with the demands of our vocation, in order to aid us to become "men crucified to the world and to whom the world itself is crucified," and thus to seek the glory of God through the salvation of souls.

Finally, I shall with your leave express my earnest hope that vernacular translations of these excerpts may appear as soon as possible and be made available to all our members. Thus all those who are striving to make progress along this "way to God" prepared by St. Ignatius will be able to gain greater familiarity with these texts, in which each of them can contemplate the model of perfection in Christ which the texts portray.

> Pedro Arrupe
> Superior General of the Society
> of Jesus

Rome, January 2, 1968
Feast of the Holy Name of Jesus

Editor's Introduction: The Spirit

A keen awareness of the life-giving spirit or tenor of thought from which St. Ignatius' *Constitutions of the Society of Jesus* sprang is probably the most important aid toward understanding and relishing them. Without that they may appear to be merely a code of statutes and rather dry.

It is, of course, also important to recall the basic facts pertaining to the terms *Examen, Constitutions,* and *Summary of the Constitutions,* and to the historical origin of these documents. These items are treated briefly on pages 87-90 below. They were placed there as an Appendix, however, lest treatment here might distract from the more important topic which is now taken up.

1. *The Life-giving Spirit within Ignatius'*
   Examen *and* Constitutions

God in his providence gradually led Ignatius of Loyola to a world view or outlook on life wonderfully inspirational both for personal sanctification and apostolic activity. Ignatius spontaneously projected that outlook into everything he did or wrote. In his *Spiritual Exercises* he applied it toward aiding an individual person to discern how he or she can fulfill God's will best for his or her particular case, and also toward motivating the person to serve God with vigor. In his *Constitutions* Ignatius applied it to the inspiration and government of an apostolic religious order. That outlook or world view, in fact, is the life-giving spirit or tenor of thought which is vibrant throughout his *Constitutions.* It is also the framework into which their separate statements or statutes must be fitted if they are to be understood aright. Hence it is useful here to recall a few salient characteristics of Ignatius' world view.

God gradually led Ignatius, largely through mystical contemplation, to a world view whereby he saw all things as proceeding from God, and then becoming a means by which man could make his way toward salvation or happiness, here and hereafter, by praising or glorifying God. God also led Ignatius to an intense desire to be associated intimately with Christ and to cooperate with him in achieving God's slowly unfolding plan of creation and redemption. Ignatius' constant hope and habitual endeavor was to make all his activities result in praise or glory to God greater than would have accrued to Him without them.

As a result, the "greater" praise or glory of God became the criterion by which he habitually made his decisions in deliberations about options confronting him. In Ignatius' usage, "glory," "praise," and "honor" to God are synonyms which constantly recur—in some 133 instances in the *Examen* and *Constitutions;* and they often overlap in meaning with the phrase "the service of God," which occurs some 140 times. At first appearance this constant recurrence might seem merely a formalistic repetition of a motto or cliché. But that is not the case, for usually the phrase used has a nuance which is functionally important in the immediate context. For example, by inserting the phrase "the greater glory of God," Ignatius is often reminding his reader of the proper criterion of deciding in a context about options. Important instances can be seen in *Constitutions,* [622,a and 623,a] below.

One prominent characteristic of his spirituality, and especially important for understanding his *Constitutions,* is his sharp focus on ends with accompanying means. His ends were hierarchically arranged (see, for example, *Constitutions,* [662 and 666] below). In large measure he was able to inspire, win, and govern men so successfully because he so clearly presented to them the inspiring goals for which he was enlisting their cooperation.

His one supreme and inspiring end, the keystone to which everything else in his arch was support, was: "the greater glory of God," with "glory" meaning praise and implying service. In his Society this single aim was to be sought by means of the members' efforts toward personal sanctification and apostolic activities. To that supreme but simple end, as Joseph de Guibert has pointed out,[1] everything else was means: material goods or evangelical poverty, work or restorative repose, even prayer itself.

Furthermore, since Ignatius regarded all the procedures and structures envisaged in his *Constitutions* as means to that supreme and simple end, the phrase "the greater praise and service of God" is mentioned constantly throughout this book as his criterion for decisions. His *Constitutions* are not merely a code of laws but also, and perhaps more importantly, a manual of discernment toward helping superiors or members to discover the better choices in the options which arise before them: Which option is likely, in the long run, to lead to greater glory of the Divine Majesty?

Inevitably, Ignatius' *Constitutions* were culturally conditioned by his times, and consequently contain a mixture of perennial principles and timely measures which were valid chiefly or even only for their own era. Since he was devising practical procedures or structures for his contemporary Jesuits in their sixteenth-century environment, some elements gradually became partially or even wholly obsolete because of the changing circumstances. To separate the perennial from the timely in his *Constitutions* (as also in his *Spiritual Exercises*) is a difficult but fruitful task for us as interpreters today. Usually, his ends for which those measures were means are still valid, and also his manner of marshalling all those intermediate ends toward his one supreme end, greater praise and service to God. In such instances, to attend carefully to his ends is generally our best means to appraise his prescriptions rightly, to draw profit from them spiritually, and to adapt them wisely to the changed circumstances of our own day.

2. *A Common Spirit in the* Exercises *and* Constitutions

It is easy to see, then, how characteristic it is of Ignatius that he begins the march of thought of his *Spiritual Exercises* by presenting for the exercitant's pondering, in the First Principle and Foundation ([23]), a clear statement of his purpose in life:

---

1 Joseph de Guibert, S.J., *The Jesuits: Their Spiritual Doctrine and Practice* (St. Louis 1972), pp. 70, 178.

> Man is created to praise, reverence, and serve God our Lord, and by this means to save his soul.
>
> And the other things on the face of the earth are created for man, that they may help him in attaining the end for which he is created.

A careful reading of Ignatius' whole "Foundation" reveals that it comprises four principal pillars, all of which are functional in supporting the structure of thought later in the *Exercises,* particularly in the Election and Rules for Discernment: (1) an attractive goal to inspire the exercitant, salvation; (2) the means, creatures rightly and wisely used; (3) a preliminary attitude, keeping onself "indifferent" or undecided until the sound reasons for a choice appear; and (4) a criterion of choice, the option which is likely to result in greater praise or glory to God. These four "pillars" of Ignatius' thought are as truly operative throughout the *Examen* and *Constitutions* as they are in the *Exercises.*

Also characteristic of him, therefore, is his beginning the *General Examen* in much the same way as the *Exercises.* After a brief statement about what the Society is, an apostolic religious institute approved by the pope, he immediately puts the Society's end before the candidate—in a formulation more direct, clear, simple, and inspiring than he has written in any other one place:

> [3]—The end of this Society is to devote itself, with God's grace, not only to the salvation and perfection of the members' own souls but also, with that same grace, to labor strenuously in giving aid toward the salvation and perfection of the souls of their fellowmen.
>
> [4]—To achieve this end more effectively, the three vows of obedience, poverty, and chastity are taken in the Society. . . .

"To achieve this end more effectively"—this phrase clearly shows that Ignatius conceived the vows as means to the Society's end just expressed. That is equally true of all the statutes, procedures, or structures which he set up in the *Examen* and *Constitutions.* To understand them aright we must keep fresh in mind their relationship as means to that inspiring end. And with this awareness we are in position to take up the readings which follow.

1. READINGS FROM
THE *GENERAL EXAMEN*

Chapter 4

Some Observances within the Society Which Are More Important for the Candidates to Know

[**53**][1]—The intention of the first men who bound themselves together in this Society should be explained to the candidates. Those founders' mind was that those received into it should be persons already detached from the world and determined to serve God totally, whether in one religious institute or another; and further, in conformity with this, that all those who seek admission into the Society should, before they begin to live under obedience in any house or college belonging to it, distribute all the temporal goods they might have, and renounce and dispose of those they might expect to receive. Further still, the founders' intention was that the candidates should carry out this distribution first in regard to matters of debt and obligation, if any existed (and in that case provision should be made as

---

1 The numbers in square brackets have been added to St. Ignatius' text by modern editors since 1949 and have now become standard.

soon as possible). In the absence of such obligations, the candidates should make the distribution in favor of pious and holy causes, according to the words, "He has scattered abroad and has given to the poor" [Ps. 111:9; 2 Cor. 9:9], and according to those of Christ, "If thou wilt be perfect, go, sell all that thou hast, and give to the poor . . . and follow me" [Matt. 19:21]—thus making that distribution according to their own devotion and casting away from themselves all hope of being able to possess those goods at any time.

*

[**61**]—Everyone who enters the Society, following the counsel of Christ our Lord that "He who leaves father" and the rest [Matt. 19:29; Luke 18:30], should judge that he should leave his father, mother, brothers, sisters, and whatever he had in the world. Even more, he should consider as spoken to himself that statement: "He who does not hate his father and mother and even his own life, cannot be my disciple" [Luke 14:26].

Consequently he should endeavor to put aside all merely natural affection for his relatives and convert it into spiritual, by loving them only with that love which right ordered charity requires. He should be as one who is dead to the world and to self-love and who lives only for Christ our Lord, while having Him in place of parents, brothers, and all things.

*

[**81**]—If he is pleased to remain in the Society, his food, drink, clothing, shoes, and lodging will be what is characteristic of the poor; and he should persuade himself that it will be what is worst in the house, for his greater abnegation and spiritual progress and to arrive at a certain quality and common norm among all. For where the Society's first members have passed through these necessities and greater bodily wants, the others who come to it should endeavor, as far as they can, to reach the same point as the earlier ones, or to go farther in our Lord.

[**82**]—The professed before making profession, the coadjutors before taking their vows, and (when the superior thinks it wise) the scholastics before becoming approved and pronouncing their vows with the promise mentioned above, should for the love of God our Lord beg from door to door for a period of three days at the times assigned them, thus imitating those earliest members. The purpose is that, contrary to common human opinion, they may be able in God's service and praise to humiliate themselves more and make greater spiritual progress, giving glory to His Divine Majesty. Another purpose is to enable them to find themselves more disposed to do the same begging when they are so commanded, or when it is expedient or necessary for them as they travel through various regions of the world, according to what the supreme vicar of Christ our Lord may order or assign to them, or, in his place, the one who will find himself superior of the Society.For our profession requires that we be prepared and very much ready for whatever is enjoined upon us in our Lord and at whatsoever time, without asking for or expecting any reward in this present and transitory life, but hoping always for that life which in its entirety is eternal, through God's supreme mercy.

[**83**]—But to come down to details, during the tests of humility and abnegation of oneself through the performance of lowly and humble tasks, such as working in the kitchen, cleaning the house, and all the rest of these services, one should take on more promptly those in which greater repugnance is found, if one has been ordered to do them.

[**84**]—When anyone begins to perform the services of the kitchen or to aid the cook, with great humility he must obey him in all things pertaining to his office, by showing him always complete obedience. For if he should not do this, neither, it seems, would he show this obedience to any other superior, since genuine obedience considers, not the person to whom it is offered, but Him for whose sake it is offered; and if it is exercised for the sake of our Creator and Lord

alone, then it is the very Lord of everything who is obeyed. In no manner, therefore, ought one to consider whether he who gives the order is the cook of the house or its superior, or one person rather than another. For, to consider the matter with sound understanding, obedience is not shown either to these persons or for their sake, but to God alone and only for the sake of God our Creator and Lord.

*

[**89**]—In time of illness one ought to observe obedience of great integrity not only toward his spiritual superiors that they may direct his soul, but also and with equal humility toward the physicians and infirmarians that they may care for his body; for the former work for his complete spiritual welfare and the latter for that which is corporal. Furthermore, the one who is sick should, by showing his great humility and patience, endeavor to give no less edification in the time of his illness to those who visit him and converse and deal with him than he does in the time of full health, for the greater glory to God.

*

[**91**]—Through reflection in our Lord, what follows has seemed good to us in His Divine Majesty. It is a matter of great and even extraordinary importance that the superiors should have a complete understanding of the subjects, that by means of it they may be able to direct and govern them better, and while looking out for the subjects' interests guide them better into the paths of the Lord.

[**92**]—Likewise, the more completely the superiors know these subjects' interior and exterior affairs, just so much the better will they be able, with greater diligence, love, and care, to help the subjects and to guard their souls from various inconveniences and dangers which might occur later on. Further still, in conformity with our profession and manner of proceeding, we should always be ready to travel about in various regions of the world, on all occasions when the supreme pontiff or our immediate superior orders us.

To proceed without error in such missions, or in sending some persons and not others, or some for one task and others for different ones, it is not only highly but even supremely important for the superior to have complete knowledge of the inclinations and motions of those who are in his charge, and to what defects or sins they have been or are more moved and inclined; that thus he may direct them better, without placing them beyond the measure of their capacity in dangers or labors greater than they could in our Lord endure with a spirit of love; and also that the superior, while keeping to himself what he learns in secret, may be better able to organize and arrange what is expedient for the whole body of the Society.

*

[101]—It is likewise highly important to bring this to the mind of those who are being examined (through their esteeming it highly and pondering it in the sight of our Creator and Lord), to how great a degree it helps and profits one in the spiritual life to abhor in its totality and not in part whatever the world loves and embraces, and to accept and desire with all possible energy whatever Christ our Lord has loved and embraced. Just as the men of the world who follow the world love and seek with such great diligence honors, fame, and esteem for a great name on earth, as the world teaches them, so those who are progressing in the spiritual life and truly following Christ our Lord love and intensely desire everything opposite. That is to say, they desire to clothe themselves with the same clothing and uniform of their Lord because of the love and reverence which He deserves, to such an extent that where there would be no offense to His Divine Majesty and no imputation of sin to the neighbor, they would wish to suffer injuries, false accusations, and affronts, and to be held and esteemed as fools (but without their giving any occasion for this), because of their desire to resemble and imitate in some manner our Creator and Lord Jesus Christ, by putting on His clothing and uniform, since it was for our spiritual profit that He clothed Himself as He did. For He gave us an

example that in all things possible to us we might seek, through the aid of His grace, to imitate and follow Him, since He is the way which leads men to life. Therefore the candidate should be asked whether he finds himself in a state of desires like these which are so salutary and fruitful for the perfection of his soul.

[102]—In a case where through human weakness and personal misery the candidate does not experience in himself such ardent desires in our Lord, he should be asked whether he has any desires to experience them. If he answers affirmatively that he does wish to have holy desires of this kind, then, that he may the better reach them in fact, he should be questioned further: Is he determined and ready to accept and suffer with patience, through the help of God's grace, any such injuries, mockeries, and affronts entailed by the wearing of this uniform of Christ our Lord, and any other affronts offered him, whether by someone inside the house or the Society (where he desires to obey, be humiliated, and gain eternal life) or outside it by any persons whatsoever on earth, while returning them not evil for evil but good for evil?

[103]—The better to arrive at this degree of perfection which is so precious in the spiritual life, his chief and most earnest endeavor should be to seek in our Lord his greater abnegation and continual mortification in all things possible; and our endeavor should be to help him in those things to the extent that our Lord gives us His grace, for His greater praise and glory.

2. READINGS FROM

THE *CONSTITUTIONS* AS SUCH

Preamble to the *Constitutions*

[**134**]—Although it must be the Supreme Wisdom and Goodness of God our Creator and Lord which will preserve, direct, and carry forward in His divine service this least Society of Jesus, just as He deigned to begin it; and although what helps most on our own part toward this end must be, more than any exterior constitution, the interior law of charity and love which the Holy Spirit writes and engraves upon hearts; nevertheless, since the gentle arrangement of Divine Providence requires cooperation from His creatures, and since too the vicar of Christ our Lord has ordered this, and since the examples given by the saints and reason itself teach us so in our Lord, we think it necessary that constitutions should be written to aid us to proceed better, in conformity with our Institute, along the path of divine service on which we have entered.

PART I

The Admission to Probation

[142]—It is highly important for the divine service to make a proper selection of those who are admitted and to take care to know their abilities and vocation well.

[143]—Both he who has the authority to admit and his helper ought to know the Society's concerns and to be zealous for its good progress, so that no other consideration will be so strong as to deter him from what he judges in our Lord to be more suitable for His divine service in this Society. Therefore he should be very moderate in his desire to admit [C].

[144]—Declaration C. Just as care should be taken to cooperate with the divine motion and vocation by endeavoring to secure in the Society an increase of workers for the holy vineyard of Christ our Lord, so too should much thought be given to admit only those who possess the qualifications required for this Institute, for the divine glory.

*

[147]—To speak in general of those who should be admitted, the greater the number of natural and infused gifts someone has from God our Lord which are useful for what the Society aims at in His divine service, and the more experience the candidate has in the use of these gifts, the more suitable will he be for reception into the Society.

Candidates for Temporal Tasks

[**148**]—To speak in particular of those who are admitted to become coadjutors in temporal or external matters, it is presupposed that they should not be more numerous than is necessary to aid the Society in occupations which the other members could not fulfill without detriment to the greater service of God. In regard to their souls these applicants ought to be men of good conscience, peaceful, docile, lovers of virtue and perfection, inclined to devotion, edifying for those inside and outside the house, content with the lot of Martha in the Society, well-disposed toward its Institute, and eager to help it for the glory of God our Lord.

[**152**]—In view of the end of our Institute and our manner of proceeding, we are convinced in our Lord that to admit persons who are very difficult or unserviceable to the congregation is not conducive to His greater service and praise, even though their admission would be useful to themselves.

Candidates for Spiritual Tasks

[**153**]—Those who are admitted to serve in spiritual matters should have the following qualifications, because of what a ministry of this kind requires for the help of souls.

[**154**]—In regard to the intellect, they should have sound doctrine, or ability to acquire it, and in respect to things to be done, discretion or evidence of good judgment which is necessary to acquire discretion.

[**155**]—In regard to the memory, they should have aptitude to learn and faithfully retain what has been learned.

[**156**]—8. In regard to the will, they should be desirous of all virtue and spiritual perfection, peaceful, constant, and energetic in whatever enterprise of the divine service they undertake, and zealous for the salvation of souls. For that

reason they should also have an affection toward our Institute, which is directly ordered to help and dispose souls to gain their ultimate end from the hand of God our Creator and Lord.

[**161**]—The extrinsic gifts of nobility, wealth, reputation, and the like, are not necessary when the others are present, just as they do not suffice if those others are lacking. But to the extent that they aid toward edification, they render more fit to be admitted those who would be fit without them because they have the other qualifications mentioned above. The more an applicant is distinguished for those qualifications the more suitable will he be for this Society unto glory of God our Lord, and the less he is distinguished by them, the less suitable. But the holy unction of the Divine Wisdom will teach [1 John 2:20, 27] the mean which should be retained in all this to those who have charge of that matter, which was undertaken for His greater service and praise.

*

[**163**]—The charity and zeal for souls in which this Society exerts itself according to the purpose of its Institute embrace all kinds of persons, to serve and help them in the Lord of all men to attain to beatitude. Nevertheless, when there is a question of incorporating persons into the same Society, that charity and zeal should embrace only those who are judged useful for the end it seeks.

PART II

The Dismissal of Those Who

Did Not Prove Themselves Fit

[204]—Just as it is proper, for the sake of the end sought in this Society, the service of God our Lord by helping souls who are His, to preserve and multiply the workers who are found fit and useful for carrying this work forward, so is it also expedient to dismiss those who are found unsuitable, and who as time passes make it evident that this is not their vocation or that their remaining in the Society does not advance the common good. However, just as excessive readiness should not be had in admitting candidates, so ought it to be used even less in dismissing them; instead, one ought to proceed with much consideration and weighing in our Lord. The more fully one has been incorporated into the Society, the more serious ought the reasons to be. Nevertheless, no matter how advanced the incorporation may be, in some cases anyone can and should be separated from the Society.

[206]—The authority to dismiss will be vested chiefly in the Society as a whole when it is assembled in a general congregation. The superior general will have the same authority in all other cases except one involving himself. The other members of the Society participate, each one, in this authority to the extent that it is communicated to them

by the head. But it is wise that it be communicated amply to the provincial superiors, and in proper proportion to those local superiors or rectors, to whom it seems good that it should be communicated, in order that the subordination arising from holy obedience may be better preserved in the whole body of the Society, in proportion to the better understanding by the members that they depend on their immediate superiors, and that for them it is highly profitable and necessary to be subject to these superiors in all things for Christ our Lord.

*

Causes for Dismissal

[**209**]—The discreet charity of the superior who has the authority to dismiss ought to ponder before God our Lord the causes which suffice for dismissal. But to speak in general, they seem to be of four kinds.

[**210**]—The first cause is present if it is perceived in the same Lord of ours that someone's remaining in this Society would be contrary to His honor and glory, because this person is judged to be incorrigible in some passions or vices which offend His Divine Majesty. The more serious and culpable these are, the less ought they to be tolerated, even though they do not scandalize the others because they are occult.

[212]—The second cause is present if it is perceived in the same Lord that to retain someone would be contrary to the good of the Society. Since this is a universal good, it ought to be preferred to the good of one individual by one who is sincerely seeking the divine service. This cause would be present if in the course of the probation some impediments or notable defects should be discovered which the applicant failed to mention earlier during the examination, or if experience should show that he would be highly unprofitable and hinder rather than aid the Society, because of his notable incompetency for any office whatever.

[**216**]—The third cause is present if one's remaining is seen to be simultaneously contrary to the good of the Society and of the individual. For example, this could arise from the body, if during the probation such illnesses and weakness are observed in someone that it seems in our Lord that he could not carry on the labor which is required in our manner of proceeding in order to serve God our Lord by that way. It could also arise from the soul, if the one who was admitted to probation is unable to bring himself to live under obedience and to adapt himself to the Society's manner of proceeding, because he is unable or does not wish to submit his own judgment, or because he has other obstacles arising from nature or habits.

[**217**]—The fourth cause is present if his remaining is seen to be contrary to the good of others outside the Society. This could arise from discovery of the bond of marriage, or of legitimate slavery, or of debts of importance, after he concealed the truth about this matter in the examination.

If any one whatsoever of these four causes exists, it seems that God our Lord will be better served by giving the person proper dismissal than by employing indiscreet charity in retaining him in whom the causes are found.

*

[**218**]—With those who must be dismissed, that manner ought to be employed which before God our Lord is likely to give greater satisfaction to the one who dismisses as well as to the one dismissed and to the others within and without the house.

PART III

The Formation of the Novices

[**243**]—Proper consideration and prudent care should be employed toward preserving in their vocation those who are being kept and tested in the houses or colleges, and toward enabling them to make progress, both in spirit and in virtues along the path of the divine service, in such a manner that there is also proper care for the health and bodily strength necessary to labor in the Lord's vineyard.

*

Spiritual Progress

[**244**]—In regard to the soul, it is of great importance to keep those who are in probation away from all imperfections and from whatever can impede their greater spiritual progress.

[**250**]—All should take special care to guard with great diligence the gates of their senses (especially the eyes, ears, and tongue) from all disorder, to preserve themselves in peace and true humility of their souls, and to give an indication of it by silence when it should be kept and, when they must speak, by the discretion and edification of their words, the modesty of their countenance, the maturity of their walk, and all their movements, without giving any sign of impatience or pride. In everything they should try and desire to give the advantage to the others, esteeming them all in their hearts as better than themselves [Phil. 2:3] and

showing exteriorly, in an unassuming and simple religious manner, the respect and reverence befitting each one's state, in such a manner that by observing one another they grow in devotion and praise God our Lord, whom each one should endeavor to recognize in his neighbor as in His image.

[251]—In the refection of the body care should be taken to observe temperance, decorum, and propriety both interior and exterior in everything. A blessing should precede the meal and a thanksgiving come after it; and all ought to recite these with proper devotion and reverence. During the meal food should also be given to the soul, through the reading of some book which is devotional rather than difficult so that all can understand it and draw profit from it, or through having someone preach during that time, according to what the superiors may order, or through doing something similar for the glory of God our Lord.

[254]—That they may begin to experience the virtue of holy poverty, all should be taught that they should not have the use of anything of their own as being their own.

[257]—Likewise they should understand that they may not lend, borrow, or dispose of anything in the house unless the superior knows it and consents.

[260]—They should be taught how to guard themselves from the illusions of the devil in their devotions and how to defend themselves from all temptations. They should know the means which can be found to overcome them and to apply themselves to the pursuit of the true and solid virtues, whether this be with many spiritual visitations or with fewer, by endeavoring always to go forward in the path of the divine service.

[261]—They should practice the daily examination of their consciences and confess and receive Communion at least every eight days, unless the superior for some reason

orders otherwise. There should be one confessor for all, assigned by him who has charge of the others. Or if this is impossible, everyone should at least have his own regular confessor to whom he should keep his conscience completely open.

[**263**]—It will be beneficial to have a faithful and competent person whose function is to instruct and teach the novices in regard to their interior and exterior conduct, to encourage them toward this correct deportment, to remind them of it, and to give them kindly admonition; a person whom all those who are in probation may love and to whom they may have recourse in their temptations and open themselves with confidence, hoping to receive from him in our Lord counsel and aid in everything. They should be advised, too, that they ought not to keep secret any temptation which they do not tell to him or their confessor or the superior, being happy that their entire soul is completely open to them. Moreover, they will tell him not only their defects but also their penances or mortifications, or their devotions and all their virtues, with a pure desire to be directed if in anything they have gone astray, and without desiring to be guided by their own judgment unless it agrees with the opinion of him whom they have in place of Christ our Lord.

[**265**]—Temptations ought to be anticipated by their opposites, for example, if someone is observed to be inclined toward pride, by exercising him in lowly matters thought fit to aid toward humbling him; and similarly of other evil inclinations.

[**269**]—In regard to the corrections and penances, the measure which ought to be observed will be left to the discreet charity of the superior and of those whom he has delegated in his place, that they may adjust them in accordance with the disposition of the persons and with the edification of each and every one of them for divine glory. Each one ought to accept them in a good spirit with a

genuine desire of his emendation and spiritual profit, even when the reason for their imposition is not that of some blameworthy defect.

[**272**]—In their illnesses all should try to draw fruit from them not only for themselves but for the edification of others. They should not be impatient nor difficult to please. Rather, they should have and show much patience and obedience to the physician and infirmarian, and employ good and edifying words which show that the sickness is accepted as a gift from the hand of our Creator and Lord, since it is a gift not less than is health.

[**273**]—As far as possible, we should all think alike and speak alike, in conformity with the Apostle's teaching [Phil. 2:2]; and differing doctrines ought not to be permitted, either orally in sermons or public lectures, or in books; (and it will not be permissible to publish books without the approval and permission of the superior general, who will entrust the examination of them to at least three persons of sound doctrine and clear judgment about the field in question). Even in regard to things which are to be done, diversity, which is generally the mother of discord and the enemy of union of wills, should be avoided as far as possible. This union and agreement among them all ought to be sought with great care and the opposite ought not to be permitted, in order that, being united among themselves by the bond of fraternal charity, they may be able better and more efficaciously to apply themselves in the service of God and the aid of their fellowmen.

[**277**]—On certain days of each week instruction should be given about Christian doctrine, the manner of making a good and fruitful confession, receiving Communion, assisting at Mass and serving it, praying, meditating, and reading [good spiritual books], in accordance with each one's capacity. Likewise, care should be taken that they learn what is proper and do not let it be forgotten, and put it into practice; that is, all of them should give time to

spiritual things and strive to acquire as much devotion as divine grace imparts to them. Toward this purpose it will help to give some of the Spiritual Exercises, or all of them, to those who have not made them, according to what is judged expedient for them in our Lord.

[282]—It will be very specially helpful to perform with all possible devotion the tasks in which humility and charity are practiced more; and, to speak in general, the more one binds himself to God our Lord and shows himself more generous[1] toward His Divine Majesty, the more will he find God more generous toward himself and the more disposed will he be to receive graces and spiritual gifts which are greater each day.

[284]—To make progress, it is very expedient and highly necessary that all should devote themselves to complete obedience, by recognizing the superior, whoever he is, as being in the place of Christ our Lord and by maintaining interior reverence and love for him. They should obey entirely and promptly, not only by exterior execution of what the superior commands, with becoming energy and humility, and without excuses and murmurings even though things are commanded which are difficult and repugnant to sensitive nature [V]; but they should try to maintain in their inmost souls genuine resignation and true abnegation of their own wills and judgments, by bringing their wills and judgments wholly into conformity with what

---

1 " . . . charity . . .; the more one binds himself to God . . . and shows himself more generous . . . ": The heart or essence of Ignatius' concept of religious life was: the total and irrevocable consecration, through love, of oneself to God. This concept of his inspiringly shines through this section [282] and his accompanying Declaration on it in [283]. Charity is the greatest virtue of the spiritual life (1 Cor. 13:13) and, as St. Thomas observes (*Summa theol.,* 2-2, q. 17, a. 6, ad 3), "charity makes us tend toward God, by uniting our affections to him, so that we live, not for ourselves but for God." And Ignatius views the religious vows as means to this total dedication, as we see in his Declaration ([283]): "To bind oneself more to God our Lord and to show oneself generous toward him is to consecrate oneself completely and irrevocably to his service, as those do who dedicate themselves to him by vow."

the superior wills and judges, in all things in which no sin is seen, and by regarding the superior's will and judgment as the rule of their own, in order to conform themselves more completely to the first and supreme rule of all good will and judgment, which is the Eternal Goodness and Wisdom.

[285]—Declaration V. It will be helpful from time to time for superiors to see to it that those who are in probation feel their obedience and poverty, by testing them for their greater spiritual progress in the manner in which God tested Abraham [Gen., ch. 22], and that they may give an example of their virtue and grow in it. But in this the superiors should as far as possible observe the measure and proportion of what each one can bear, as discretion will dictate.

[286]—That they may exercise themselves more in obedience, it is good and likewise highly necessary that they should obey not only the superior of the Society or house, but also the subordinate officials who hold their authority from him, in regard to everything for which that authority over them was given. They should accustom themselves to consider not who the person is whom they obey, but rather who He is for whose sake they obey and whom they obey in all, who is Christ our Lord.

[287]—All should love poverty as a mother, and according to the measure of holy discretion all should, when occasions arise, feel some effects of it. Further, as is stated in the Examen [53-59], after the first year they should be ready, each one, to dispose of their temporal goods whenever the superior may command it, in the manner which was explained to them in the aforementioned Examen.

[288]—All should make diligent efforts to keep their intention right, not only in regard to their state of life but also in all particular details. In these they should always aim at serving and pleasing the Divine Goodness for its own

sake and because of the incomparable love and benefits with which God has anticipated us, rather than for fear of punishments or hope of rewards, although they ought to draw help also from them. Further, they should often be exhorted to seek God our Lord in all things, stripping off from themselves the love of creatures to the extent that this is possible, in order to turn their love upon the Creator of them, by loving Him in all creatures and all of them in Him, in conformity with His holy and divine will.

*

Care of the Body

[292]—Just as an excessive preoccupation over the needs of the body is blameworthy, so too a proper concern about the preservation of one's health and bodily strength for the divine service is praiseworthy, and all should exercise it. Consequently, when they perceive that something is harmful to them or that something else is necessary in regard to their diet, clothing, living quarters, office or the manner of carrying it out, and similarly of other matters, all ought to inform the superior about it or the one whom he appoints. But meanwhile they should observe two things. First, before informing him they should recollect themselves to pray, and after this, if they perceive that they ought to represent the matter to him who is in charge, they should do it. Second, after they have represented it by word of mouth or by a short note as a precaution against his forgetting it, they should leave the whole care of the matter to him and regard what he ordains as better, without arguing or insisting upon it either themselves or through another, whether he grants the request or not [A]. For the subject must persuade himself that what the superior decides after being informed is more suitable for the divine service and the subject's own greater good in our Lord.

[293]—Declaration A. Even though the subject who represents his need ought not personally to argue or urge the matter, nevertheless if the superior has not yet

understood it, and if he requests further explanation, the subject will give it. If by chance he forgets to provide after he has indicated his intention to do so, it is not out of order to recall it to his memory or to represent it with becoming modesty.

[**300**]—The chastisement of the body ought not to be immoderate or indiscreet in abstinences, vigils, and other external penances and labors which damage and impede greater goods. Therefore it is expedient for each one to keep his confessor informed of what he does in this matter. If the confessor thinks that there is excess or has a doubt, he should refer the matter to the superior. All this is done that the procedure may be attended by greater light and God our Lord may be more glorified through our souls and bodies.

PART IV

The Formation of the Scholastics

[308]—A. The aim and end of this Society is, by traveling through the various regions of the world at the order of the supreme vicar of Christ our Lord or of the superior of the Society itself, to preach, hear confessions, and use all the other means it can with the grace of God to help souls. Consequently it has seemed necessary to us, or at least highly expedient, that those who will enter the Society should be persons of good life and sufficient learning for the aforementioned work. But in comparison with others, those who are both good and learned are few; and even among these few, most of them already seek rest from their previous labors. As a result, the increase of the Society from such men of letters who are both good and learned is, we find, something very difficult to achieve, because of the great labors and the great abnegation of oneself which are required in the Society.

Therefore all of us, desiring to preserve and develop the Society for greater glory and service to God our Lord have thought it wise to proceed by another path. That is, our procedure will be to admit young men who because of their good habits of life and ability give hope that they will become both virtuous and learned in order to labor in the vineyard of Christ our Lord.

*

Formation in Studies

[**339**]—What was stated in Part III will suffice about the care and welfare, in regard to the body and external matters, of those who live in the colleges. That is, special attention should be given to their abstaining from studies at times inopportune for bodily health, to their taking sufficient sleep, and to their observance of moderation in mental labors, that they may have greater endurance in them both during the years of study and later on in using what they have studied for the glory of God our Lord.

[**340**]—In regard to spiritual matters, the same order of procedure will be used with those who are received in the colleges, as long as they are still going through probations, as that which is observed with those who are received in the houses. But after they have been approved and while they are applying themselves to their studies, just as care must be taken that through fervor in study they do not grow cool in their love of true virtues and of religious life, so also during that time there will not be much place for mortifications and long prayers and meditations. For their devoting themselves to learning, which they acquire with a pure intention of serving God and which in a certain way requires the whole man, will be not less but rather more pleasing to God our Lord during this time of study.

[**346**]—For greater devotion, and to refresh the memory of the obligation they are under, and to confirm themselves more solidly in their vocation, it will be good for the scholastics twice each year to renew their simple vows, using the formula given in Part V, Chapter 4.

[**360**]—In order to make great progress in their studies, the scholastics should strive first of all to keep their souls pure and their intention in studying right, by seeking in their studies nothing except the glory of God and the good of souls. Moreover, they should frequently beg in prayer for grace to make progress in learning for the sake of this end.

[**361**]—Furthermore, they should keep their resolution firm to be thoroughly genuine and earnest students, by persuading themselves that while they are in the colleges they cannot do anything more pleasing to God our Lord than to study with the intention mentioned above; likewise, that even if they never have occasion to employ the matter studied, their very labor in studying, taken up as it ought to be because of charity and obedience, is itself work highly meritorious in the sight of the Divine and Supreme Majesty.

[**362**]—The impediments which distract from study should also be removed, both those arising from devotions and mortifications which are too numerous or without proper order and also those springing from their cares and exterior occupations whether in duties inside the house or outside it in conversations, confessions, and other activities with one's fellowmen, as far as it is possible in our Lord to excuse oneself from them. For in order that the scholastics may be able to help their fellowmen better later on by what they have learned, it is wise to postpone exercises such as these, pious though they are, until after the years of study, since there will be others to attend to them in the meantime. All this should be done with a greater intention of service and divine glory.

The Means of Helping One's Fellowmen

[**400**]—In view of the objective which the Society seeks by means of its studies, toward the end of them it is good for the scholastics to begin to accustom themselves to the spritual arms which they must employ in aiding their fellowmen; and this work can be begun in the colleges, even though it is more properly and extensively done in the houses.

[**401**]—First of all, those who in the judgment of the superior should be ordained are to be taught how to say Mass not only with interior understanding and devotion but

also with an exterior manner good for the edification of those who hear the Mass. All the members of the Society should as far as possible use the same uniform ceremonies, by conforming themselves in them, as far as the diversity of regions permits, to the Roman usage as the one which is more universal and embraced in a special way by the Apostolic See.

[**402**]—Similarly, they will exercise themselves in preaching and in delivering [sacred] lectures in a manner suitable for the edification of the people, which is different from the scholastic manner, by endeavoring to learn the [vernacular] language well, to have, as matters previously studied and ready at hand, the means which are more useful for this ministry, and to avail themselves of all appropriate means to perform it better and with greater fruit for souls.

[**406**]—They should also practice themselves in the administration of the sacraments of confession and Communion, by keeping fresh in mind and endeavoring to put into practice not merely what pertains to themselves, but also what pertains to the penitents and communicants, that they may receive and frequent these sacraments well and fruitfully for divine glory.

[**408**]—After they have had experience of the Spiritual Exercises in their own selves, they should acquire experience in giving them to others. Each one should know how to give an explanation of them and how to employ this spiritual weapon, since it is obvious that God our Lord has made it so effective for His service [E].

[**409**]—Declaration E. They could begin by giving the Exercises to some in whose cases less is risked, and by conferring about their method of procedure with someone more experienced, noting well what he finds more useful and what less so. Their explanation of the Exercises should be given in such a manner that it does not merely give satisfaction to the others but also moves them to desire to be

helped by the Exercises. Generally, only the exercises of the first week should be given. When they are given in their entirety, this should be done with outstanding persons or with those who desire to decide upon their state of life.

[410]—They should likewise bestow appropriate study upon the method of teaching Christian doctrine and of adapting themselves to the capacities of children or simple persons.

[412]—Just as one's fellowmen are helped to live well by what has been stated above, so an effort should be made to know what helps them to die well and what procedure should be used at a moment so important for gaining or losing the ultimate end, eternal happiness.

[414]—In general, they ought to be instructed about the manner of acting proper to a member of the Society, who has to associate with so great a diversity of persons throughout such varied regions. Hence they should foresee the inconveniences which may arise and the opportunities which can be grasped for the greater service of God, by using some means at one time and others at another. Although all this can be taught only by the unction of the Holy Spirit [1 John 2:20, 27] and by the prudence which God our Lord communicates to those who trust in His Divine Majesty, nevertheless the way can at least be opened by some suggestions which aid and dispose one for the effect which must be produced by divine grace.

*

The Character of the Rector

[423]—Care should be taken that the rector be a man of great example, edification, and mortification of all his evil inclinations, and one especially approved in regard to his obedience and humility. He ought likewise to be discreet, fit for governing, experienced both in matters of business and

of the spiritual life. He should know how to mingle severity with kindness at the proper times. He should be solicitous, stalwart under work, a man of learning, and finally, one in whom the higher superiors can confide and to whom they can with security delegate their authority. For the greater this delegated authority will be, the better will the colleges be governed for greater divine glory.

[**424**]—The function of the rector will be first of all to sustain the whole college by his prayer and holy desires, and then to bring it about that the Constitutions are observed [B]. He should watch over all his subjects with great care, and guard them against difficulties from within or without the house by anticipating the difficulties and remedying them if they have occurred, in the way that seems conducive to the good of the individuals and to that of all. He should strive to promote their progress in virtues and learning, and care for their health and for the temporal goods both stable and movable. He should appoint officials discreetly, observe how they proceed, and retain them in office or change them as he judges appropriate in the Lord. In general he ought to see to it that what has been stated about the colleges in the preceding chapters is carried out.

He should observe in its entirety the submission he ought to maintain not merely toward the superior general but also to the provincial superior, by keeping him informed and having recourse to him in the matters of greater moment, and by following the order given him, since the provincial is his superior, in the same way as those of his own college should act toward him. His subjects ought to hold him in great respect and reverence as one who holds the place of Christ our Lord, while leaving to him with true obedience the free disposal of themselves and their affairs, not keeping anything closed to him, not even their own conscience. Rather, as has been stated in the Examen [93-97], they should manifest their conscience to him at fixed times, and more frequently when there is reason, without showing any repugnance or any manifestations of contrary opinion, that by the union of their opinion and will with his and by proper submission they may be better preserved and make greater progress in the divine service.

[**425**]—Declaration B. Thus just as it will pertain to the rector to endeavor to have the Constitutions observed in their entirety, so it will be his to grant dispensations from them with authority from his own superiors, when he judges that such would be the intention of the one who composed them, in a particular case according to occurrences and necessities and while keeping his attention fixed on the greater common good.

[**434**]—The rector should endeavor that all those in the college practice an integral obedience to each official in his own office, and these officials to the minister and to the rector himself, in accordance with the order which he prescribes to them. Ordinarily those who have charge of others who must obey them ought to give them an example by the obedience which they themselves observe to their own superiors as persons holding the place of Christ our Lord.

[**435**]—A suitable order of time for study, prayer, Masses, lectures, eating and sleeping, and so on, will be helpful for everything. Thus a signal will be given at designated times. When it is heard, all should go immediately, leaving even a letter they have begun. When these hours ought to be changed because of the seasons or other unusual reasons, the rector or the one in charge should consider the matter and what he orders should be observed.

PART V

Incorporation into the Society

[**510**]—Those who have been tested in the Society sufficiently and for a time long enough that both parties may know whether their remaining in it is conducive to greater service and glory to God our Lord, ought to be admitted, not to probation as was the case in the beginning, but in a more intrinsic manner as members of one same body of the Society.

[**516**]—Since no one should be admitted unless he has been judged fit in our Lord, for admission to profession those persons will be judged worthy whose life is well-known through long and thorough probations and is approved by the superior general, to whom a report will be sent by the other superiors or others from whom the general desires information.

For this purpose, after those who were sent to studies have achieved the diligent and careful formation of the intellect by learning, they will find it helpful during the period of the last probation to apply themselves in the school of the heart, by exercising themselves in spiritual and corporal pursuits which can engender in them greater humility, abnegation of all sensual love and will and judgment of their own, and also greater knowledge and love of God our Lord; that when they themselves have made progress they can better help others to progress for glory to God our Lord.

[520]—In addition to these, some can be admitted to the profession of only three solemn vows. But this will be done rarely and for special and important reasons. These members should have been known in the Society for seven years during which they have given in it great satisfaction by their talent and virtues, for glory to God our Lord.

[522]—To be admitted among the formed coadjutors, a subject should likewise have given satisfaction in regard to his life and good example and his ability to aid the Society, either in spiritual matters by his learning or in exterior matters without the learning, each one according to what God has communicated to him. By his discretion the superior general will have to appraise this matter too, unless it seems good to him to entrust it to the particular persons in whom he has much confidence in our Lord.

[523]—That subjects may be admitted among the approved scholastics, proportionately the same set of requirements remains. Especially in regard to their ability, there should be hope that they will succeed in their duties, in the judgment of the general or of the one whom he designates while confiding in the discretion and goodness which God our Lord has given to him.

PART VI

The Religious Life of Those Incorporated

[547]—In order that those already admitted to profession or to membership among the formed coadjutors may be able to apply themselves more fruitfully according to our Institute in the service of God and the aid of their fellowmen, they themselves ought to observe certain things.

*

What pertains to the vow of chastity does not require explanation, since it is evident how perfectly it should be preserved through the endeavor in this matter to imitate the angelic purity by the purity of the body and mind. Therefore, with this presupposed, we shall now treat of holy obedience.

*

Obedience

All should keep their resolution firm to observe obedience and to distinguish themselves in it, not only in the matters of obligation but also in the others, even though nothing else is perceived except the indication of the superior's will without an expressed command. They should keep in view God our Creator and Lord, for whom such obedience is practiced, and they should endeavor to proceed in a spirit of love and not as men troubled by fear. Hence all of us should exert ourselves not to miss any point of perfection which we can with God's grace attain in the observance of all the Constitutions and in our manner of proceeding in our Lord, by applying all our energies with very special care to the virtue of obedience shown first to the sovereign pontiff and then to the superiors of the Society.

Consequently, in all the things into which obedience can with charity be extended [B], we should be ready to receive its command just as if it were coming from Christ our Savior, since we are practicing the obedience to one in His place and because of love and reverence for Him. Therefore we should be ready to leave unfinished any letter or anything else of ours which has been begun and to apply our whole mind and all the energy we have in the Lord of all that our obedience may be perfect in every detail [C], in regard to the execution, the willing, and the understanding. We should perform with great alacrity, spiritual joy, and perseverance whatever has been commanded to us, persuading ourselves that everything is just and renouncing with blind obedience any contrary opinion and judgment of our own in all things which the superior commands and in which (as it was stated [284]) some species of sin cannot be judged to be present. We ought to be firmly convinced that everyone of those who live under obedience ought to allow himself to be carried and directed by Divine Providence through the agency of the superior as if he were a lifeless body which allows itself to be carried to any place and to be treated in any manner desired, or as if he were an old man's staff which serves in any place and in any manner whatsoever in which the holder wishes to use it. For in this way the obedient man ought joyfully to devote himself to any task whatsoever in which the superior desires to employ him to aid the whole body of the religious Institute; and he ought to hold it as certain that by this procedure he is conforming himself with the divine will more than by anything else he could do while following his own will and different judgment.

[549]—Declaration B. Such things are all those in which some sin is not manifest.

[550]—Declaration C. The command of obedience is fulfilled in regard to the execution when the thing commanded is done; in regard to the willing when the one who obeys wills the same thing as the one who commands; in regard to the understanding when he forms the same judgment as the one commanding and regards what he is commanded as good. And that obedience is imperfect in which there does not exist, in addition to the execution, also that agreement in willing and judging between him who commands and him who obeys.

[551]—Likewise, it should be strongly recommended to all that they should have and show great reverence, especially interior reverence, to their superiors, by considering and reverencing Jesus Christ in them; and from their hearts they should warmly love their superiors as fathers in Him. Thus in everything they should proceed in a spirit of charity, keeping nothing exterior or interior hidden from the superiors and desiring them to be informed about everything, in order that the superiors may be the better able to direct them in everything along the path of salvation and perfection. For that reason, once a year and as many times more as their superior thinks good, all the professed and formed coadjutors should be ready to manifest their consciences to him, in confession, or secret, or in another manner, for the sake of the great profit this practice contains, as was stated in the Examen [91, 92, 97]. Thus too they should be ready to make a general confession, from the last one they made, to the one whom the superior thinks it wise to designate in his place.

*

Poverty

[553]—Poverty, as the strong wall of the religious life, should be loved and preserved in its integrity as far as this is possible with God's grace. The enemy of the human race generally tries to weaken this defense and rampart which God our Lord inspired religious institutes to raise against him and the other adversaries of their perfection. Into what

was well ordered by their first founders he induces alterations by means of interpretations and innovations not in conformity with those founders' spirit. Therefore, that provision may be made in this matter as far as lies in our power, all those who make profession in this Society should promise not to take part in altering what pertains to poverty in the Constitutions, unless it be in some manner to make it more strict, according to the circumstances in the Lord.

[565]—All who are under the obedience of the Society should remember that they ought to give gratuitously what they have gratuitously received [Matt. 10:9], without demanding or accepting any stipend or alms in recompense for Masses or confessions or preaching or lecturing or visiting or any other ministry among those which the Society may exercise according to our Institute, that thus it may proceed in the divine service with greater liberty and greater edification of the neighbor.

[570]—Just as no personal possession may be held in the house, so neither may one be held outside the house in the hands of another. Each one should be content with what is given to him from the common supply for his necessary or proper use, without any superfluity.

[580]—What pertains to food, sleep, and the use of the other things necessary or proper for living, will be ordinary and not different from that which appears good to the physician of the region where one lives, in such a manner that what each one subtracts from this will be withdrawn through his own devotion and not through obligation. Nevertheless there should be concern for the humility, poverty, and spiritual edification which we ought to keep always in view in our Lord.

*

Personal Spiritual Life

[582]—In view of the time and approval of their life

through which those wait before being admitted among the professed and even among the formed coadjutors, it is presupposed that they will be men who are spiritual and sufficiently advanced to run in the path of Christ our Lord to the extent that their bodily strength and the exterior occupations undertaken through charity and obedience allow. Therefore, in what pertains to prayer, meditation, and study and also in regard to the bodily practices of fasts, vigils, and other austerities or penances, it does not seem expedient to give them any other rule than that which discreet charity dictates to them [A], provided that the confessor should always be informed and also, when a doubt about expediency arises, the superior. The following statement is the only one which will be made in general. On the one hand, the members should keep themselves alert that the excessive use of these practices may not weaken the bodily energies and consume time to such an extent that these energies are insufficient for the spiritual help of one's fellowmen according to our Institute; and on the other hand, they should be vigilant that these practices may not be relaxed to such an extent that the spirit grows cold and the human and lower passions grow warm.

[583]—Declaration A. If the superior thinks it expedient to give some subjects a determined time to keep them from being either excessive or deficient in their spiritual exercises, he will have the authority to do this. So too in regard to the use of the other means, if he judges in some case that one of these means ought to be employed without leaving this matter to the discretion of the individual, he will proceed in accordance with what God our Lord leads him to think proper. And the part of the subject will be to accept with complete devotion the order which is given to him.

*

Aiding Our Fellowmen

[586]—Because the occupations which are undertaken for the aid of souls are of great importance, proper to our Institute, and very frequent; and because, on the other

hand, our residence in one place or another is so highly uncertain, our members will not regularly hold choir for the canonical hours or sing Masses and offices. For one who experiences devotion in listening to those chanted services will suffer no lack of places where he can find his satisfaction; and it is expedient that our members should apply their efforts to the pursuits that are more proper to our vocation, for glory to God our Lord.

[**588**]—Likewise, because the members of this Society ought to be ready at any hour to go to some or other parts of the world where they may be sent by the sovereign pontiff or their own superiors, they ought not to take a curacy of souls, and still less ought they to take charge of religious women or any other women whatever to be their confessors regularly or to direct them. However, nothing prohibits them in passing from hearing the confessions of a whole monastery for special reasons.

*

Those Who Die in the Society

[**595**]—Both during his whole life and also and even more at the time of his death, each member of the Society ought to strive earnestly that through him God our Lord may be glorified and served and his fellowmen may be edified, at least by the example of his patience and fortitude along with his living faith, hope, and love of the eternal goods which Christ our Lord merited and acquired for us by those altogether incomparable sufferings of His temporal life and death. But sickness is often such that it greatly impairs the use of the mental faculties; and through the vehement attacks of the devil and the great importance of not succumbing to him, the passing away is itself such that the sick man needs help from fraternal charity. Therefore with great vigilance the superior should see to it that the one who in the physician's opinion is in danger should, before being deprived of his judgment, receive all the holy sacraments and fortify himself for the passage from this temporal life to

that which is eternal, by means of the arms which the divine liberality of Christ our Lord offers.

*

The Constitutions Not Obligatory under Pain of Sin

[**602**]—The Society desires that all the Constitutions and Declarations and its regime of living should be observed in every regard according to our Institute, without deviation in anything; and on the other hand it also desires that its individual members may be free from anxiety or aided against falling into any snare of sin which could arise through the obligation of these Constitutions or ordinations. For that reason our considered opinion in our Lord is that, apart from the express vow which the Society has with respect to the currently reigning sovereign pontiff, and apart from the other three essential vows of poverty, chastity, and obedience, no constitutions, declarations, or regime of living can oblige under mortal or venial sin, unless the superior orders the subjects in the name of our Lord Jesus Christ or in virtue of obedience, which may be done in regard to things and persons where it is judged to be highly expedient for the particular good of each one or for the universal good. Thus in place of the fear of giving offense there should arise a love and desire of all perfection, and a desire that greater glory and praise of Christ our Creator and Lord may follow.

PART VII

Distribution of the Incorporated Members in the Vineyard of Christ

[603]—Part VII deals with the members' duties toward their fellowmen (which is an end eminently characteristic of our Institute) when these members are dispersed to any part of Christ's vineyard, to labor in that part of it and in that work which have been entrusted to them. They may be sent to some places or others by the supreme vicar of Christ our Lord, or by the superiors of the Society, who for them are similarly in the place of His Divine Majesty; or they themselves may choose where and in what work they will labor, when they have been commissioned to travel to any place where they judge that greater service of God and the good of souls will follow; or they may carry on their labor, not by traveling but by residing steadily and continually in certain places where much fruit of glory and service to God is expected.

*

Missions from the Holy Father

Since one's being sent on a mission of His Holiness will be treated first, as being most important, it should be observed that the vow which the Society made to obey him as the supreme vicar of Christ without any excuse, meant that the members were to go to any place whatsoever where he judges it expedient to send them for the greater glory of

God and the good of souls, whether among the faithful or the infidels [B]. The Society did not mean any particular place, but rather that it was to be distributed into diverse regions and places throughout the world, and it desired to proceed more correctly in this matter by leaving the distribution of its members to the sovereign pontiff.

[**605**]—Declaration B. The intention of the fourth vow pertaining to the pope was not to designate a particular place but to have the members distributed throughout the various parts of the world. For those who first united to form the Society were from different provinces and realms and did not know into which regions they were to go, whether among the faithful or the unbelievers; and therefore, to avoid erring in the path of the Lord, they made that promise or vow in order that His Holiness might distribute them for greater glory to God. They did this in conformity with their intention to travel throughout the world and, when they could not find the desired spiritual fruit in one region, to pass on to another and another, ever intent on seeking the greater glory of God our Lord and the greater aid of souls.

[**606**]—In this matter, the Society has placed its own judgment and desire under that of Christ our Lord and His vicar; and neither the superior for himself nor any individual member of the Society will be able for himself or for another to arrange or to try to arrange, directly or indirectly, with the pope or his ministers to reside in or to be sent rather to one place than another. The individual members will leave this entire concern to the supreme vicar of Christ and to their own superior; and in regard to his own person the superior will in our Lord leave this concern to His Holiness and to the Society.

[**609**]—Moreover, he who has been designated by His Holiness to go to some region should offer his person generously, without requesting provisions for the journey or causing a request for anything temporal to be made, except

that His Holiness should order the member to be sent in the manner that His Holiness judges to be a greater service of God and of the Apostolic See, without taking thought about anything else.

[**616**]—When the residence in determined places must be prolonged and when it is possible without prejudice to the principal mission and intention of the sovereign pontiff, it will not be improper for the one on the mission to make some excursions to aid the souls in the neighboring regions and afterwards to return to his residence, if such excursions are possible and it appears to him that they could be fruitful in service to God our Lord. Likewise in the territory where he resides, he ought to attend with special care to the charge which was especially given to him and not to neglect it for other opportunities in the divine service, even good ones. Yet in addition to that charge he can and he ought to consider, but without prejudice to his mission, as has been said, in what other things he can employ himself for the glory of God and the good of souls. Thus he does not lose the opportunity for this which God sends him, to the extent that he will judge expedient in the Lord.

*

Missions from the Superior of the Society

[**618**]—To be able to meet the spiritual needs of souls in many regions with greater facility and with greater security for those who go among them for this purpose [A], the superiors of the Society, according to the faculty granted by the sovereign pontiff, will have authority to send any of the Society's members whomsoever [B] to whatsoever place these superiors think it more expedient to send them [C], although these members, wherever they are, will always be at the disposition of His Holiness.

However, there are many who request help while considering more their own spiritual obligations to their flocks, or other advantages not so immediately their own, rather than the common or universal benefits. Therefore the superior general, or whoever holds this authority from him, ought to bestow much careful thought on missions of this kind in order that, when he sends subjects to one region rather than to another [D], or for one purpose rather than for another [E], or one particular person rather than another or several of them [F], in this manner or in that [G], for a greater or lesser time [H], that procedure may always be used which is conducive to the greater service of God and the universal good.

If the superior thinks, while holding fast to this thoroughly right and pure intention in the presence of God our Lord, that it is wise because of the difficulty or importance of the decision, he will commend the matter to His Divine Majesty and cause it to be commended in the prayers and Masses of the house. He will also discuss it with one or more members of the Society who happen to be present and whom he thinks suitable. Then he himself will decide about sending or not sending, and about the other circumstances, as he will judge to be expedient for greater glory to God.

The part of him who is sent will be, without interposing himself in favor of going or remaining in one place rather than another, to leave the disposition of himself completely and freely to the superior who in the place of Christ our Lord directs him in the path of His greater service and praise [I]. In similar manner, too, no one ought to try by any means to bring it about that others will remain in one place or go to another, unless he does so with the approval of his superior, by whom he should be governed in our Lord [K].

[619]—Declaration A. The superior of the Society can more easily and more expeditiously make provision for many places (especially those remote from the Apostolic See), than would be the case if those who need members of the Society must always approach the sovereign pontiff. For the individual members, too, there is greater security if they go from obedience to their superiors rather than through their own decision (even if they were capable of making it),

and not as men sent by him whom they have in place of Christ to direct them as the interpreter of His divine will.

[**620**]—Declaration B. Just as the general can perform the other functions by himself and through persons under him, so too can he perform this one of sending his subjects on missions, by reserving to himself the missions which he thinks should be thus reserved.

[**621**]—Declaration C. The sending of subjects "to whatsoever place these superiors think it expedient" means either among the faithful, even though it be in the Indies, or among the unbelievers, especially where there is a colony of believers, as in Greece and elsewhere. Where the inhabitants are more exclusively unbelievers, the superior should ponder seriously in the sight of God our Lord whether he ought to send subjects or not, and where, and whom. The part of the subject will always be to accept his appointment joyfully as something from God our Lord.

The Choice of Places

[**622, a**]—Declaration D. To proceed more successfully in this sending of subjects to one place or another, one should keep the greater service of God and the more universal good before his eyes as the norm to hold oneself on the right course.[1] It appears that in the vineyard of the Lord, which is so extensive, the following procedure of selection ought to be used. When other considerations are equal (and this should be understood in everything that follows), that part of the vineyard ought to be chosen which has greater need, because of the lack of other workers or because of this misery and weakness of one's fellowmen in it and the danger of their eternal condemnation.

---

1 This statement, so typical of Ignatius and of his outlook on life (see p. 18 above), is his simple and fundamental criterion for choosing ministries; and all that follows in *Cons,* [622,b—634] is an application of this criterion to varying cases or details—as we readily see if we recall that greater service to God also brings greater glory to him (*Cons,* [603, 609]).

[**b**]. Consideration should also be given to where the greater fruit will probably be reaped through the means which the Society uses. This case would arise, for example, where one sees the door more widely open and a better disposition among the people along with compliancy favorable to their progress. This disposition consists in the people's greater devotion and desire (which can be judged in part by the insistence they show), or in the condition and quality of the persons who are more capable of making progress and of preserving the fruit produced, to the glory of God our Savior.

[**c**]. In places where our indebtedness is greater, for example, where there is a house or college of the Society or where there are members of it who study and are the recipients of charitable deeds from those people, and when it is granted that the other considerations pertaining to spiritual progress are equal, it would be more fitting to have some laborers there, and for that reason to prefer these places to others, in conformity with perfect charity.

[**d**]. The more universal the good is, the more is it divine. Therefore preference ought to be given to those persons and places which, through their own improvement, become a cause which can spread the good accomplished to many others who are under their influence or take guidance from them.

[**e**]. For that reason, the spiritual aid which is given to important and public persons ought to be regarded as more important, since it is a more universal good. This is true whether these persons are laymen such as princes, lords, magistrates, or ministers of justice, or whether they are clerics such as prelates. The same also holds true of the spiritual aid which is given to persons distinguished for learning and authority, because of that reason of its being the more universal good. For that same reason, too, preference ought to be shown to the aid which is given to the great nations such as the Indies, or to important cities, or to universities, which are generally attended by numerous persons who by being aided themselves can become laborers for the help of others.

[**f**]. Similarly, the Society ought to labor more intensely in those places where the enemy of Christ our Lord has sown cockle [Matt. 13:24-30], and especially where he has spread bad opinion about the Society or stirred up ill will against it so as to impede the fruit which the Society could produce. This is especially to be observed if the place is an important one of which account should be taken, by sending there, if possible, persons such that by their life and learning they may undo the evil opinion founded on false reports.

The Choice of Undertakings

[**623, a**]—Declaration E. For better success in the choice of undertakings for which the superior sends his subjects, the same norm should be kept in view, namely, that of considering the greater divine honor and the greater universal good. This consideration can supply completely just reasons for sending a subject to one place rather than to another. To touch upon some motives which can exist in favor of one place or another, we mention these.

[**b**]. First of all, the members of the Society may occupy themselves in undertakings directed toward benefits for the soul, and also in those directed toward benefits for the body through the practice of mercy and charity. Similarly, they may help some persons in matters pertaining to their greater perfection, or to their lesser perfection; and finally, in regard to things which are of themselves of more good, or of less good. In all these cases, if both things cannot be done simultaneously and the other considerations are equal, the spiritual goods ought to be preferred to the bodily, the matters of greater perfection to those of less, and the things more good to those less good.

[**c**]. Likewise, when there are some things in the service of God our Lord which are more urgent, and others which are less pressing and can better suffer postponement of the remedy, even though they are of equal importance, the first ought to be preferred to the second.

[**d**]. Similarly too, when there are some things which are especially incumbent upon the Society or it is

seen that there are no others to attend to them, and other things in regard to which others do have care and a method of providing for them, in choosing missions there is reason to prefer the first to the second.

[e]. Likewise also, among the pious works of equal importance, urgency, and need, when some are safer for the one who cares for them and others are more dangerous; and when some are easier and more quickly dispatched and others are more difficult and finished only in a longer time, the first should be similarly preferred over the second.

[f]. When everything mentioned above is equal and when there are some occupations which are of more universal good and extend to the aid of more of our fellowmen, such as preaching or lecturing, and others which are concerned more with individuals, such as hearing confessions or giving Exercises; and when further it is impossible to accomplish both sets of occupations simultaneously, preference should be given to the first set, unless there should be some circumstances through which it would be judged that to take up the second set would be more expedient.

[g]. Similarly too, when there are some spiritual works which continue longer and are of more lasting value, such as certain pious foundations for the aid of our fellowmen, and other works less durable which give help on a few occasions and only for a short while, then it is certain that the first ought to be preferred to the second. Hence it is also certain that the superior of the Society ought to employ his subjects more in the first type rather than in the second, since that is a greater service to God and a greater good for our fellowmen.

The Choice of Persons

[624, a]—Declaration F. Although it is the supreme providence and direction of the Holy Spirit that must efficaciously guide us to bring deliberations to a right conclusion in everything, and in sending to each place those who are more suitable and who will fit in better with the men

and work to which they are sent, still this can be said in general. First, that for a matter of greater importance and one in which more depends on avoidance of error, as far as this depends on the part of the one who with God's grace must provide, subjects ought to be sent who are more select and in whom greater confidence is had.

[**b**]. In matters which involve greater bodily labors, persons more strong and healthy.

[**c**]. In matters which contain greater spiritual dangers, persons more approved in virtue and more reliable.

[**d**]. To go to discreet persons who hold posts of spiritual or temporal government, those members seem most suitable who excel in discretion and grace of conversation and (while not lacking interior qualities), have a pleasing appearance which increases their prestige. For their counsel can be highly important.

[**e**]. To treat with cultivated persons of talent and learning, those are more suitable who likewise have a special gift of skill and learning. For these persons can be more successful in lectures and conversations.

[**f**]. For the ordinary people, those will generally be most apt who have talent for preaching, hearing confessions, and the like.

[**g**]. The number and combination of such laborers who are to be sent should also receive consideration. First of all, it would be wise when possible that one member should not be sent alone. At least two should be sent, that thus they may be more helpful to one another in spiritual and bodily matters and also, by distributing among themselves the labors in the service of their neighbor, be more profitable to those to whom they are sent.

[**h**]. And if two set out, it seems that with a preacher or lecturer there could well go another who in confessions and spiritual exercises could gather in the harvest which the speaker prepares for him, and who could aid the speaker by conversations and the other means used in dealing with our fellowmen.

[**i**]. Likewise, when one less experienced in the

Society's manner of proceeding and of dealing with the neighbor is sent, it seems that he ought to be accompanied by another who has more experience in that procedure, whom he can imitate, with whom he can confer, and from whom he can take counsel in the perplexing matters which he encounters.

[**j**]. With one very ardent and daring it seems that there could well go another more circumspect and cautious. Procedure similar to this, too, could be used in regard to other combinations, in such wise that the diversity may, when united by the bond of charity, be helpful to both of them and may not engender contradiction or discord, either among them or with their fellowmen.

[**k**]. To send more than two when the importance of the work intended in the service of God our Lord is greater and requires a larger number, and when the Society can provide more laborers without prejudice to other things conducive to greater divine glory and universal good, is something which the superior will have authority to do, accordingly as the unction of the Holy Spirit inspires him [1 John 2:20, 27] or as he judges in the sight of His Divine Majesty to be better and more expedient.

[**625**]—G. In regard to the manner in which he is to send them (after the proper instruction), the superior should deliberate whether he will send them in the manner of the poor, so that they would go on foot and without money, or with better facilities; whether with letters to be helpful toward winning acceptance and benevolence at their destination; and whether these letters should be addressed to individuals, or the city, or its head. In regard to all the details, the superior will consider the greater edification of the neighbor and the service of God our Lord and then decide what should be done.

[**626**]—H. When no limitation has been set by the sovereign pontiff as regards the time for which some laborers are sent to one place and others to another, it seems

that the length of their stay ought to be regulated by the following considerations. Thought should be given to the nature of the spiritual affairs being dealt with, to the greater or less importance the men themselves have as viewed against the need and the fruit which is being reaped or expected. Then, too, attention must be given to the opportunities available in other places, to the obligation there is to take up these works, and to the resources which the Society possesses to provide for these other undertakings. One should also weigh the accidents which can intervene to shorten or prolong the time. Finally, one should attend to the first characteristic of our Institute. Since this is to travel through some regions and others, remaining for a shorter or longer time in proportion to the fruit which is seen, it will be necessary to judge whether it is expedient to give more time or less to certain missions or to others. That this may be perceived, it is important that those who are sent should keep the superior informed by frequent reports about the fruit which is reaped.

When it is necessary to change someone, the superior should remember that in recalling him he should, as far as possible, use such means that those from among whom he is taken will retain all their benevolence rather than suffer a certain disedification, being persuaded that in everything the honor and glory of God and the universal good are being sought.

[627]—I. For someone to propose the motions or thoughts which occur to him contrary to an order received, meanwhile submitting his entire judgment and will to the judgment and will of his superior who is in the place of Christ, is not against this prescription.

[628]—K. By this it is clearly forbidden that any member should influence some prince, or community, or person of authority to write a request to the superior for some member of the Society or to ask this of him by word of mouth, unless the member has first communicated the

matter to the superior and understood this procedure to be his will.

*

A Member's Free Movement

[633]—It is the part of those who live under obedience to the Society not to scheme, directly or indirectly, to be sent here or there, either by His Holiness or by their own superior in the name of Christ our Lord. Nevertheless one who is sent to an extensive region such as the Indies or other provinces and for whom no particular district is marked out, may remain in one place for a longer or shorter period. Or, after considering the reasons on one side and the other, while praying and keeping his will indifferent, he may travel about wherever he judges this to be more expedient for the glory of God our Lord.

From this it is clear that, without swerving from that foremost and supreme order of His Holiness, in missions of this type the superior will have much greater power to direct a member to one place rather than another, as he judges in the Lord to be expedient.

[634]—Wherever anyone is stationed, if he is not limited to the use of some means such as lecturing or preaching, he may use the means which he judges more suitable among those which the Society employs. They have been mentoned in Part IV [402-414] and will be mentioned again in the following chapter. Similarly, he will avoid what those passages disapprove, for greater service to God.

*

How the Houses and Colleges
Can Help Their Fellowmen

[636]—Since the Society endeavors to aid its fellowmen not merely by traveling through diverse regions but also by residing continually in some places, for example, in the houses and colleges, it is important to have learned the ways in which souls can be helped in those places, in order to use

that selection of these ways which is possible for the glory of God our Lord.

[**637**]—The first way that comes to mind is the good example of a thoroughly upright life and of Christian virtue, through the effort to edify by good deeds no less but rather more than by words those with whom one deals.

[**638**]—Likewise, the neighbor is aided by desires in the presence of God our Lord and by prayers for all the Church, especially for those persons in it who are of greater importance for the common good [A]. They should also pray for friends and benefactors, living and dead, whether they request these prayers or not. Similarly, let them pray for those for whose special benefit they and the other members of the Society are working in diverse places among believers or unbelievers, that God may dispose them all to receive His grace through the feeble instruments of this least Society.

[**639**]—Declaration A. Examples of such persons are the ecclesiastical princes, the secular princes, and other persons who have great power to promote or impede the good of souls and the divine service.

[**642**]—Further still, the neighbor can be aided through the administration of the sacraments, especially the hearing of confessions (with some priests being assigned by the superior for this service) and through administering Holy Communion, apart from the Communion of Easter time received in the communicant's parish church.

[**645**]—In the church the word of God should be proposed to the people unremittingly by means of sermons, lectures, and the teaching of Christian doctrine, by those whom the superior approves and designates for this work, and at the times and in the manner which he judges to be most conducive to greater divine glory and edification of souls [E].

[**646**]—Declaration E. Since it could happen in some places that on some occasion it is not expedient to employ these means or some part of them, this constitution does not oblige except when the superior thinks that these means should be used. However, it shows the Society's intention in the places where it will have a domicile, namely, that use should be made of all three of these means of proposing God's words, or two of them, or that one which seems more suitable.

[**647**]—The same procedure described above may also be followed outside the Society's church, in other churches, squares, or places of the region, when the one in charge judges it expedient for God's greater glory.

[**648**]—Likewise, they will endeavor to be profitable to individuals by spiritual conversations, by counseling and exhorting to good works, and by conducting Spiritual Exercises [F].

[**649**]—F. The Spiritual Exercises should not be given in their entirety except to a few persons, namely, those of such a character that from their progress notable fruit is expected for the glory of God. But the exercises of the first week can be made available to large numbers; and some examinations of conscience and methods of prayer (especially the first of those which are touched on in the Exercises) can also be given far more widely; for anyone who has good will seems to be capable of these exercises.

[**650**]—The members will also occupy themselves in corporal works of mercy to the extent that the more important spiritual activities permit and their own energies allow. For example, they can help the sick, especially those in hospitals, by visiting them and by sending others to serve them. They can reconcile the disaffected and do what they can for the poor and for prisoners in the jails, both by their personal work and by getting others to do it. How

much of all this it is expedient to do will be regulated by the discretion of the superior, who will keep always in view the greater service of God and the universal good.

PART VIII

The Union of the Members

[**655**]—The more difficult it is for the members of this congregation to be united with their head and among themselves, since they are so scattered among the faithful and among the unbelievers in diverse regions of the world [A], the more ought means to be sought for that union. For the Society cannot be preserved, or governed, or, consequently, attain the end it seeks for the greater glory of God unless its members are united among themselves and with their head. Therefore the present treatise will deal first with what can aid the union of hearts and later with helps toward the union of persons in congregations or chapters. With respect to the union of hearts, some of the helpful means lie on the side of the subjects, others on the side of the superiors, and others on both sides.

[**656**]—Declaration A. There are also other reasons, for example, the fact that ordinarily they will be learned men, that they will have the favor of princes or important persons, or of peoples, and so forth.

The Part of the Members

[**657**]—On the side of the subjects, it will be helpful neither to admit a large crowd of persons to profession nor to retain any other than select persons even as formed coadjutors or scholastics [B]. For a large number of persons

whose vices are not well mortified is an obstruction to order and that union which is in Christ our Lord so necessary for the preservation of this Society's good condition and manner of proceeding.

[**658**]—Declaration B. This does not exclude the number, even though it is very large, of persons who are suitable for profession or for the formed coadjutors or the approved scholastics. But it recommends avoidance of leniency in regarding as fit those who are not, especially for admission among the professed. When that which was stated in Part I and Part V is well observed, enough will be done. For a group of members of that quality, even if it is numerous, is not to be regarded as a crowd, but as an elite race.

[**659**]—Since this union is produced in great part by the bond of obedience, this virtue should always be maintained in its vigor; and those who are sent out from the houses to labor in the Lord's field should as far as possible be persons practiced in this virtue. Those who are more important in the Society should give a good example of obedience to the others, by being closely united to their own superior and by obeying him promptly, humbly, and devoutly. Thus too one who has not given a good example of this virtue ought at least to go in the company of someone who has given it; because in general a companion more advanced in obedience will help one who is less so, with the divine favor. And even when this purpose does not exist, a collateral associate can be given to one who is sent with some charge, if the superior thinks that thus the one entrusted with this charge will carry out better what has been entrusted to him. The collateral will conduct himself in such a manner with him who has the charge, and he in turn with the collateral, that neither the obedience nor the reverence of the others is weakened; and also in such a manner that the one in authority has in his collateral a true and faithful aid as well as an alleviation for himself and for the others who are in his charge.

[**662**]—To this same virtue of obedience is related the properly observed subordination of the superiors, one to another, and of the subjects to the superiors, in such wise that the individuals dwelling in some house or college have recourse to their local superior or rector and are governed by him in every respect. Those who are distributed throughout the province refer to the provincial or some other local superior who is closer, according to the orders they received; and all the local superiors or rectors should communicate often with the provincial and thus too be directed by him in everything; and the provincials in their turn will deal in the same way with the general. For this subordination, when well observed in this manner, will preserve the union[1] which is attained chiefly through it, with the help of the grace of God our Lord.

[**664**]—One who is seen to be a cause of division among those who live together, estranging them either among themselves or from their head, ought with great diligence to be separated from that community, as a pestilence which can infect it seriously if a remedy is not quickly applied [F].

[**665**]—Declaration F. To separate can mean either to expel the person from the Society completely or to transfer him to another place, if this seems sufficient and more expedient for the divine service and the common good, in the judgment of him who has charge of the matter.

*

The Part of the Superior General

[**666**]—On the side of the superior general, that which will aid toward this union of hearts consists in the qualities of his person [G]. They will be treated in Part IX [723-725]. With them he will carry on his office, which is to be

---

1 Ignatius' hierarchically arranged series of superiors through which authority to govern descends from God, and the function of this series in furthering unity, appear very clearly in this constitution [662], as also in [666].

for all the members a head from whom descends to all of them the impulse necessary for the end which the Society seeks. Thus it is that from the general as the head flows all the authority of the provincials, and from the provincials that of the local superiors, and from that of these local superiors that of the individual members. Thus too from that same head come the assignments to missions; or at least they come by his mandate and approval. The same should be understood about the communication of the graces of the Society; for the more the subjects are dependent upon their superiors, the better will the love, obedience, and union among them be preserved.

[**667**]—Declaration G. Among other qualities, his good reputation and prestige among his subjects will be very specially helpful; and so will his having and manifesting love and concern for them, in such a way that the subjects hold the opinion that their superior has the knowledge, desire, and ability to rule them well in our Lord. For this and many other matters he will find it profitable to have with him persons able to give good counsel, as will be stated in Part IX [803, 804], whose help he can use in what he must order for the Society's good manner of proceeding in diverse regions, unto divine glory.

Further help will be found in his having his method of commanding well thought out and organized, through his endeavoring to maintain obedience in the subjects in such a manner that the superior on his part uses all the love and modesty and charity possible in our Lord, so that the subjects can dispose themselves to have always toward their superiors greater love than fear, even though both are useful at times. He can also do this by referring some matters to them when it appears probable that they will be helped by this; and at other times, by going along with them to some extent and sympathizing with them when this, it seems, could be more expedient.

*

The Bond of Charity

[671]—The chief bond to cement the union of the members among themselves and with their head is, on both sides, the love of God our Lord. For when the superior and the subjects are closely united to His Divine and Supreme Goodness, they will very easily be united among themselves, through that same love which will descend from the Divine Goodness and spread to all other men, and particularly into the body of the Society. Thus from both sides charity will come to further this union between superiors and subjects, and in general all goodness and virtues through which one proceeds in conformity with the spirit. Consequently there will also come total contempt of temporal things, in regard to which self-love, the chief enemy of this union and universal good, frequently induces disorder.

Still another great help can be found in uniformity, both interior uniformity of doctrine, judgments, and wills, as far as this is possible, and exterior uniformity in respect to clothing, ceremonies of the Mass, and other such matters, to the extent that the different qualities of persons, places, and the like, permit.

[673]—Still another very special help will be found in the exchange of letters between the subjects and the superiors, through which they learn about one another frequently and hear the news and reports which come from the various regions. The superiors, especially the general and the provincials, will take charge of this, by providing an arrangement through which each region can learn from the others whatever promotes mutual consolation and edification in our Lord.

PART IX

The Society's Head and His Government

[**719**]—In all well-organized communities or congregations there must be, besides the persons who take care of the particular goals, one or several whose proper duty is to attend to the universal good. So too in this Society, in addition to those who have charge of its single houses or colleges and of its single provinces where it has those houses or colleges, there must be someone who holds that charge of the entire body of the Society, one whose duty is the good government, preservation, and development of the whole body of the Society; and this person is the superior general.

*

The Character of the Superior General

[**723**]—In regard to the qualities which are desirable in this superior general,[1] the first is that he should be closely united with God our Lord and intimate with Him in prayer and all his actions, that from God, the fountain of all good, the general may so much the better obtain for the whole body of the Society a large share of His gifts and graces, and also great power and efficacy for all the means which will be used for the help of souls.

---

1 Ignatius' ideal of the character of the superior general, as portrayed in *Cons*, [723-735], is also largely applicable to every member of the Society (with obvious changes in detail).

[725]—The second quality is that he should be a person whose example in the practice of all virtues is a help to the other members of the Society. Charity should be especially resplendent in him, toward all his fellowmen and above all toward the members of the Society; and genuine humility too should shine forth, that these characteristics may make him highly lovable to God our Lord and to men.

[726]—He ought also to be independent of all passions, by his keeping them controlled and mortified, so that in his interior they may not disturb the judgment of his intellect and in his exterior he may be so composed, particularly so self-controlled when speaking, that no one, whether a member of the Society who should regard him as a mirror and model, or an extern, may observe in him any thing or word which does not edify him.

[727]—However, he should know how to mingle rectitude and necessary severity with kindness and gentleness to such an extent that he neither allows himself to swerve from what he judges to be more pleasing to God our Lord nor ceases to have proper sympathy for his sons. Thus although they are being reprimanded or punished, they will recognize that in what he does he is proceeding rightly in our Lord and with charity, even though it is against their liking according to the lower man.

[728]—Magnanimity and fortitude of soul are likewise highly necessary for him to bear the weaknesses of many, to initiate great undertakings in the service of God our Lord, and to persevere in them with constancy when it is called for, without losing courage in the face of the contradictions (even though they come from persons of high rank and power) and without allowing himself to be moved by their entreaties or threats from what reason and the divine service require. He should be superior to all eventualities, without letting himself be exalted by those which succeed or depressed by those which go poorly, being altogether ready

to receive death, if necessary, for the good of the Society in the service of Jesus Christ, God and our Lord.

[**729**]—The third quality is that he ought to be endowed with great understanding and judgment, in order that this talent may not fail him either in the speculative or the practical matters which may arise. And although learning is highly necessary for one who will have so many learned men in his charge, still more necessary is prudence along with experience in spiritual and interior matters, that he may be able to discern the various spirits and to give counsel and remedies to so many who will have spiritual necessities.

He also needs discretion in exterior matters and a manner of handling such diverse affairs as well as of conversing with such various persons from within and without the Society.

[**730**]—The fourth quality, one highly necessary for the execution of business, is that he should be vigilant and solicitous to undertake enterprises as well as energetic in carrying them through to their completion and perfection, rather than careless and remiss in such a way that he leaves them begun but not finished.

[**731**]—The fifth quality has reference to the body. In regard to health, appearance, and age, on the one hand account should be taken of propriety and prestige, and on the other hand of the physical energies which his charge requires, that in it he may be able to fulfill his office to the glory of God our Lord.

[**733**]—The sixth quality pertains to extrinsic endowments. Among these, preference ought to be given to those which help more toward edification and the service of God in such a charge. Examples are generally found in reputation, high esteem, and whatever else aids toward prestige with those within and without.

[**735**]—Finally, he ought to be one of those who are most outstanding in every virtue, most deserving in the Society,

and known as such for a considerable time. If any of the aforementioned qualities should be wanting, there should at least be no lack of great probity and of love for the Society, nor of good judgment accompanied by sound learning. For in regard to other things, the aids which he will have (and which will be treated below [789-808]) could through God's help and favor supply to a great extent for many deficiencies.

*

The Authority of the Superior General

[736]—It is judged altogether proper for the good government of the Society that the superior general should have complete authority over it, in order to build it up. This authority (from which the general's functions also become manifest) is that described below.

First of all, the superior general will have the power to admit, personally and through others, those whom he thinks suitable for the Institute of the Society into the houses and colleges or anywhere else. He may admit them thus to probation as well as to profession and to membership as formed coadjutors and approved scholastics. Similarly, he will have power to permit them to depart and to dismiss them.

[746]—Just as it pertains to the general to see to it that the Constitutions of the Society are observed in all places, so too he will have power to grant dispensations in particular cases which require such dispensation, while he takes account of the persons, places, times, and other circumstances. He will use this power with the discretion which the Eternal Light gives him, meanwhile keeping his attention fixed on the purpose of the Constitutions, which is the greater divine service and the good of those who live in this Institute. He may use this power in what pertains to the experiences of those who are in probation, as also in other matters where such dispensation is judged to be the intention of those who enacted the Constitutions, for the glory of God our Lord.

[**749**]—The same general will also have complete authority over the missions, but in no case may he obstruct missions of the Apostolic See, as is stated in Part VII [618]. From among those who are under his obedience he may send all, professed or not professed, to any regions of the world, for the time which seems good to him, whether it is definite or indefinite, in order to exercise any of the means which the Society uses to aid its fellowmen. Similarly, he may recall those sent, acting in everything as he judges to be conducive to the greater glory to God our Lord.

Knowing the talent of those who are under his obedience, he should distribute the offices of preachers, lecturers, confessors, and the like, by assigning each subject to the office which he judges in our Lord to be more expedient for the divine service and the good of souls.

*

[**811**]—Declaration I. From what has been said about the general it will be possible to infer what is applicable to the provincial superiors, local superiors, and rectors of colleges, with respect to their qualities, authority, function, and the aids which each one ought to have. It will be possible to state all this expressly in the rules which pertain to each of these superiors.

PART X

The Preservation and Development of the Society

[812]—The Society was not instituted by human means; and neither is it through them that it can be preserved and developed, but through the omnipotent hand of Christ, God and our Lord. Therefore in Him alone must be placed the hope that He will preserve and carry forward what He deigned to begin for His service and praise and for the aid of souls. In conformity with this hope, the first and best proportioned means will be the prayers and Masses.

[813]—For the preservation and development not only of the body or exterior of the Society but also of its spirit, and for the attainment of the objective it seeks, which is to aid souls to reach their ultimate and supernatural end, the means which unite the human instrument with God and so dispose it that it may be wielded dexterously by His divine hand are more effective than those which equip it in relation to men. Such means are, for example, goodness and virtue, and especially charity, and a pure intention of the divine service, and familiarity with God our Lord in spiritual exercises of devotion, and sincere zeal for souls for the sake of glory to Him who created and redeemed them and not for any other benefit. Thus it appears that care should be taken in general that all the members of the Society may devote themselves to the solid and perfect virtues and to spiritual pursuits, and attach greater importance to them than to

learning and other natural and human gifts. For they are the interior gifts which make those exterior means effective toward the end which is sought.

[**814**]—When based upon this foundation, the natural means which equip the human instrument of God our Lord to deal with his fellowmen will all be helps toward the preservation and development of this whole body, provided they are acquired and exercised for the divine service alone; employed, indeed, not that we may put our confidence in them, but that we may cooperate with the divine grace according to the arrangement of the sovereign providence of God our Lord. For He desires to be glorified both through the natural means, which He gives as Creator, and through the supernatural means, which He gives as the Author of grace. Therefore the human or acquired means ought to be sought with diligence, especially well-grounded and solid learning, and a method of proposing it to the people by means of sermons, lectures, and the art of dealing and conversing with men.

[**816**]—Since poverty is like a bulwark of religious institutes which preserves them in their existence and discipline and defends them from many enemies; and since the devil uses corresponding effort to destroy this bulwark in one way or another, it will be highly important for the preservation and development of this whole body that every appearance of avarice should be banished afar.

[**819**]—Much aid is given toward perpetuating the well-being of this whole body by what was said in Part I [142-144], Part II [204], and Part V [516-523] about avoiding the admission of a crowd, or of persons unsuitable for our Institute, even to probation, and about dismissals during the time of probation when it is found that some persons do not turn out to be suitable. Much less ought those to be retained who are addicted to vice or are incorrigible. But even greater strictness should be shown in admitting persons among the approved scholastics and formed coadjutors, and

strictness far greater still in regard to admission to profession. The profession should be made only by persons who are selected for their spirit and learning thoroughly and lengthily tested, and known with edification and satisfaction to all after various proofs of virtue and abnegation of themselves. This procedure is used that, even though the numbers are multiplied, the spirit may not be diminished or weakened, when those who are incorporated into the Society are such as have been described.

*

[820]—Since the well-being or illness of the head has its consequences in the whole body, it is supremely important that the election of the superior general be carried out as directed in Part IX [723-735]. Next in importance is the choice of the Society. For in a general way, the subjects will be what these superiors are.

It is also highly important that, in addition to that choice, the individual superiors should have much authority over the subjects, and the general over the individual superiors; and, on the other hand, that the Society have much authority over the general, as is explained in Part IX [736, 757, 759, 766-788]. This arrangement is made that all may have full power for good and that, if they do poorly, they may be kept under complete control.

It is similarly important that the superiors have suitable ministers, as was said in the same Part [798-810], for the organization and execution of the affairs pertaining to their office.

[821]—Whatever helps toward the union of the members of this Society among themselves and with their head will also help much toward preserving the well-being of the Society. This is especially the case with the bond of wills, which is the mutual charity and love they have for one another. This bond is strengthened by their getting information and news from one another and by having much intercommunication, by their following one same doctrine, and by their being uniform in everything as far as possible,

85

and above all by the link of obedience, which unites the individuals with their superiors, and the local superiors among themselves and with the provincials, and both the local superiors and provincials with the general, in such a way that the subordination of some to others is diligently preserved.

[**822**]—Temperate restraint in spiritual and bodily labors and similar moderation in relation to the Constitutions, which do not lean toward an extreme of rigor or toward excessive laxity (and thus they can be better observed) will help this entire body to persevere in its good state and to be maintained in it.

[**823**]—Toward the same purpose it is helpful in general to strive to retain the good will and charity of all, even of those outside the Society, and especially of those whose favorable or unfavorable attitude toward it is of great importance for opening or closing the gate leading to the service of God and the good of souls. It is also helpful that in the Society there should neither be nor be seen partiality to one side or another among Christian princes or rulers, but in its stead a universal love which embraces in our Lord all parties (even though they are adversaries to one another).

[**826**]—It will also be helpful that attention should be devoted to the preservation of the health of the individual members , as was stated in Part III [292-306]; and finally, that all should apply themselves to the observance of the Constitutions. For this purpose they must know them, at least those which pertain to each one. Therefore each one should read or hear them every month.

APPENDIX

The *Examen,* the *Constitutions*

and the *Summary of the Constitutions*

1. *The Terminology*

Through a usage dating at least from 1558, the term "Constitutions" is taken in a comprehensive sense which includes four books left still in manuscript by St. Ignatius when he died in 1556: (1) the General Examen; (2) the Declarations, authoritative explanations of the Examen; (3) the Constitutions of the Society of Jesus, the main body of his statutes (with "Constitutions" taken here in a more particularized sense); and (4) the Declarations on the Constitutions. These four books, which possess equal juridical force, were approved by General Congregation I in 1558 and thus became the Society's law, determining the papally approved Formula of the Institute in greater detail. In printed editions (designated here by italicized titles), the four treatises are usually combined to form one book.

2. *The* General Examen

The *General Examen,* a "means of investigation," is a treatise which Ignatius intended to be handed to candidates to give them a concise but accurate summary of the Society's

Institute, that is, of its manner of living and the documents in which that life is authoritatively set forth. The Examen was also a manual which aided the Society's examiner who explained and discussed it. The word General in the title applies fully only to the first four chapters, since the last four deal with particular cases. The nature of the Examen can be briefly shown by the titles of its chapters:

1. The Institute of the Society of Jesus and the diversity of its members
2. Some cases about which a candidate to the Society should be questioned
3. Some questions to gain a better knowledge of the candidate
4. Some observances within the Society which are more important for the candidate to know

[Particularized Examens]

5. Another Examen, somewhat more particularized, for the educated, the spiritual coadjutors, and the scholastics
6. Another Examen, for coadjutors alone
7. Another Examen, for scholastics . . .
8. Another Examen, for those still indifferent

3. *The* Constitutions *as Such*

The *Constitutions* (in the particularized sense of this term), the longest and most important of Ignatius' four books on government, is the main body of statutes which he composed to found, inspire, unite, and govern the members of his religious institute. Its statements expand, apply, and further determine the provisions found in the papal Formula of the Institute. In the *Constitutions* Ignatius did not aim at presenting a comprehensive treatise which, proceeding according to an order of logical thought, "first considers the end [of a religious institute] and then descends to the means to attain it." Instead, he used a practical "order of execution" which traced the stages through which a candidate would pass until he would be a member definitively incorporated and contributing his part to the unity and effective functioning of a worldwide apostolic body.[1] In an order loosely chronological, Ignatius traced in ten "parts" or chapters a candidate's admission, spiritual training as a novice, intellectual formation as a scholastic, final incorporation into the Society, and application to its work (Parts I-VII); then the union of the members among themselves and with their head (VIII), the superior general and his government (IX), and lastly a summary on the preservation and development of the Society as a whole (X).

4. *The* Summary of the Constitutions

Ignatius expressed his hope that all Jesuits would know the *Constitutions,* "at least those which pertain to each one," and that "therefore each one should read or hear them every month" ([827; see also 20]). To facilitate this familiarity, from 1553 onward successive collections of excerpts from the *General Examen* and *Constitutions* arose with the title of "Summary of the Constitutions." In 1590 Father General Mercurian promulgated a revision which bore the title *A Summary of Those Constitutions and Rules Which Pertain to the Spiritual Formation of Ours and Are to Be Observed by All.* The excerpts were well chosen. But they were arranged in a new sequence which removed them from their original contexts in Ignatius' *Constitutions* as a whole. This was an impediment to accuracy of interpretation. Passages which he had intended for novices were now applied, under the new title, to "all." These passages were indeed relevant for all, but with different nuances for novices and the experienced professed. Further still, the printed books which contained the *Summary* usually had no introductions aiding readers to fit the excerpts into their proper context in the framework of Ignatius' outlook as a whole. This too made it more difficult, especially as memory of his personality faded with the passing of centuries, to grasp his full thought with accuracy and depth. The printed books usually contained, right after the *Summary,* also the "Common Rules," on which see pages 99-100 below.

---

1 *Cons,* [137].

By an accident of history, the rules or constitutions of most new congregations of religious women who in their foundation received help from Jesuits were based on this *Summary of the Constitutions,* rather than on St. Ignatius' *Constitutions* as a whole.[2] Two exceptions to this are Mary Ward in her endeavors to found the Institute of the Blessed Virgin Mary in the 1590s and Cornelia Connelly in her founding of the Society of the Holy Child Jesus in the United States, 1846-1849.

Through some four centuries this *Summary of the Constitutions* and also the "Common Rules" were usually read at table every month in Jesuit communities. With only slight revisions it remained official in the Society until the 31st General Congregation, which in 1966 recommended new measures to make the *Constitutions* themselves better known to Jesuits today (see *DocsGC31and32,* pages 35 and 187). Consequently on January 2, 1968, Father Arrupe issued the new collection of excerpts from the *Constitutions* which are found above on pages 21-86. They are drawn from chapter 4 of the *General Examen* and all ten Parts of the *Constitutions,* and they retain the same sequence which they had in St. Ignatius' own texts.

---

2 For more on this topic, see Sister Caritas McCarthy, I.H.C.J., "Constitutions for Apostolic Religious," *Supplement 14* to *The Way* (autumn, 1971), pp. 33-45.

PART II: ADAPTATION OF THE FOUNDER'S CHARISM TO MODERN TIMES

A. *JESUIT RELIGIOUS LIFE*

A Summary of Orientations and Norms
on Our Manner of Life,
Personal and Communitarian,
as Excerpted from the Decrees of
General Congregations 31 and 32
and from Letters of
Father General Pedro Arrupe

PREFACE BY FATHER PEDRO ARRUPE

Dear Fathers and Brothers,
        The Peace of Christ.

Although the 32nd General Congregation abrogated the Common Rules, it nevertheless recommended to Father General that "at his discretion he publish a summary of the decrees of the 31st and 32nd General Congregations, together with a summary of the letters he has written to the Society since the 31st General Congregation. This summary," the Congregation added, "can serve as an index of the principal features of our religious life."[1]

In implementation of that recommendation, I now address to the whole Society the present collection of readings on our religious life, personal and communitarian. It is made up of two parts:

I. Orientations. This is a selection, by no means exhaustive, of excerpts of particular importance for guiding our reflection on the chief aspects of our religious life; and

II. Norms and practical directives. Under this head are collected the principal norms decreed by the last two General Congregations for application to the whole Society.

This summary does not contain everything. Matters pertaining to the formation of our young men, for example, must be sought in the decrees of the respective Congregations. To state the matter more generally, this summary does not dispense us from a deeper knowledge of the Decrees and Instructions; and we must have recourse to these documents themselves whenever we need a more com-

---

1 General Congregation 32, Decree 11, no. 54 [255] (hereafter abbreviated GC 32, D. 11, no. 54 [255]).

The numbers in square brackets after references to GC 31 and 32, (here, for example, the [255]), refer to the marginal numbers in the one-volume edition published by the Jesuit Conference, Washington, D.C., in 1977: *Documents of the 31st and 32nd General Congregations of the Society of Jesus.*

plete understanding of their various aspects. But the special aim of the present brief presentation in handy form is to provide a text for frequent reading.

Hence I strongly recommend this frequent reading to all, both in private and in community—especially during times of the Spiritual Exercises, spiritual recollections, and community meetings of any kind.

A further hope is that the publication of this summary may become an occasion for all to revert to frequent and meditative reading of another collection of excerpts which is of even greater importance for our religious life: the booklet entitled *Readings from the Constitutions of the Society of Jesus,* which I offered to the Society on November 6, 1967, "to facilitate a personal and deep knowledge of the Constitutions."

My counsels here do not refer to a reading which is merely routine. My conviction is that we cannot grasp the deeper meaning of the Constitutions and the Decrees of the General Congregations unless we read their key texts frequently and meditatively. Only in this way shall we grasp—as is our duty—the demands of our vocation.

Permit me to repeat, therefore, what I wrote at the close of the 31st General Congregation: "Let us not too easily think that we know these matters well enough; and let us not fear to contemplate our mission in all its amplitude."[2]

I commend myself to the prayers of all the Society's members.

> Devotedly yours in Christ,
> Pedro Arrupe
> General of the Society of Jesus

Rome, December 31, 1975

---

2 *Acta Romana Societatis Iesu* (hereafter abbreviated *ActRSJ*), XV (1967-1972), 27.

JESUIT RELIGIOUS LIFE

CONTENTS

C. OBEDIENCE

IV. UNION AND COMMUNITY

Editor's Introduction

All the readings found earlier in this book have pertained to the primitive spirit or charism of the Jesuit Institute. As we enter Part II we pass to official documents which reflect the Society's efforts to adjust that spirit to the changed circumstances of modern times. A bird's-eye view of these endeavors can be obtained from the booklet which Father General Arrupe presented to the Society on December 31, 1975, with the title *Jesuit Religious Life (De vita religiosa in Societate Iesu)*. The roots of this booklet are found in the early "Common Rules" which usually were printed within the books entitled *Summary of the Constitutions*.

1. The "Common Rules"

In *Constitutions* [136] St. Ignatius expressed his desire that his single "constitutions" should deal with matters more important, permanent, and applicable in all times and places; but that there should also be other "ordinances or rules" which could be more readily adapted to different times, places, persons, and circumstances. During his lifetime he issued many sets of such directives, which reveal his skill as an organizer securing willing cooperation and coordinated procedure from his associates. Some of them dealt with particular offices, for example, those of the sacristan, infirmarian, or cook.[1] Others were "common" to all the members of some given community; an example from 1549 is Ignatius' "Common Rules of the House."[2]

---

1 *Cons,* [428]; see also *Cons*MHSJ, IV, 175, 182, 189.

2 *Cons*MHSJ, IV, 160-168.

2. *The New Booklet* Jesuit Religious Life

Just as successive collections entitled a *Summary of the Constitutions* gradually appeared among the early Jesuits, so did similar collections carrying the title of "Common Rules." Noteworthy collections were those of 1551, 1553, 1560, 1567, and 1580. In 1616 a definitive edition was issued by General Congregation VII, shortly after the death of Father General Aquaviva.[3] These Common Rules remained substantially unchanged until 1966, when the 31st General Congregation found them poorly suited to modern times. However, the Congregation found itself unable in the available time to produce a satisfactory substitute, so it entrusted this task to Father General.[4] But committees which he appointed for this work again found themselves unable to achieve a satisfying result. Hence the 32nd General Congregation abrogated the older Common Rules, and recommended to Father General "that at his discretion he publish a *summary* of the decrees of the 31st and 32nd General Congregations together with a summary of the letters he has written to the Society since the 31st General Congregation. This summary can serve as an index of the principal features of our religious life."[5] Father Arrupe completed this task when he sent out on December 31, 1975 the booklet of which the English translation follows immediately below.

3 See *Cons*MHSJ, IV, 3*, 158, 284, 332, 555; *InstSJ*, II, 10-13.
4 *DocsGC31and32*, pp. 35, 183-186.
5 Ibid., p. 484.

A. *JESUIT RELIGIOUS LIFE*

PART I

ORIENTATIONS

INTRODUCTION

1. *A Life Inseparably Apostolic and Religious*

Since the goal to which the Society directly tends is "to help our own souls and the souls of our neighbor to attain the ultimate end for which they were created," it is necessary that our life—of priests as well as scholastics and brothers—be undividedly apostolic and religious. This intimate connection between the religious and apostolic aspects in the Society ought to animate our whole way of living, praying, and working, and impress on it an apostolic character.[3]

★

The grace of Christ that enables and impels us to seek "the salvation and perfection of souls"—or what might be called, in contemporary terms, the total and integral liberation of man, leading to participation in the life of God himself—is the same grace by which we are enabled and impelled to seek "our own salvation and perfection."[4]

---

3 GC 31, D. 13, no. 3 [204], citing *Constitutions of the Society of Jesus* (hereafter abbreviated *Cons*), [307].

4 GC 32, D. 2, no. 11 [21], citing the Formula of the Institute (hereafter abbreviated FI), [3] (1), found on p. 66 in *The Constitutions of the Society of Jesus, Translated . . .* by George E. Ganss, S.J., and also *Cons,* [3], ibid. p. 77.

These present excerpts cannot include all that pertains to the Society's apostolic works themselves, or to its apostolic orientations of the present day; on these, see especially GC 31, Decrees 3 and 31-36, and GC 32, D. 4. Nevertheless, here and there within the present excerpts indications will be found of the intimate relation between a Jesuit's personal and community life and his apostolate. Moreover, the "fundamental experience" already mentioned can truly be called the fountainhead from which a Jesuit's life and mission, in all their aspects, spring.

I. THE FUNDAMENTAL EXPERIENCE FROM WHICH THE MISSION AND LIFE OF A JESUIT SPRING

2. *The Spiritual Exercises*

The history of the Society has its beginnings in the Spiritual Exercises which our holy father Ignatius and his companions went through. . . . They had heard the invitation of Christ the King and had followed it; for that reason they not only dedicated themselves entirely to labor, but desiring to become outstanding in every service of their king, they made offerings of greater worth and importance; so that they would be "sent" under the banner of Christ by him into the entire world, spreading his teachings among all degrees and conditions of men.[5]

Ignatius and his first companions, through the spiritual experience of the Exercises, sought to look upon the world from the same apostolic point of view, in order to discover its needs. They contemplated "the three Divine Persons looking down on the surface and circuit of the globe so full of men" and deciding "that the Second Person would become man to save mankind." Then they turned their eyes to where God's gaze was fixed, and saw for themselves the men and women of their time "in all their variety of appearance and behavior: some white, others black; some at peace, others at war; some weeping, others laughing; some well, others ill; some being born, others dying; etc." That was how they learned how to respond to the call of Christ and to work for the establishment of his kingdom.[6]

To maintain faithfully the grace of our vocation as described in the Institute, the Spiritual Exercises of our holy

---

5 GC 31, D. 1, no. 2 [3]. See also St. Ignatius' *Spiritual Exercises,* (hereafter abbreviated *SpEx*), [97, 167], and his Deliberation on Poverty, no. 13, found in *Cons*MHSJ, I, 80.

6 GC 32, D. 4, no. 14 [63], citing from *SpEx,* [91-100] on the Kingdom of Christ and [102-106] on the Incarnation.

founder stand in first place, both as a perennial source of those interior gifts upon which depends our effectiveness in reaching the goal set before us, and as the living expression of the Ignatian spirit which must temper and interpret all our laws.[7]

For in the Exercises we shall continually renew our faith and our apostolic hope in reviewing our experience of the love of God in Christ Jesus. We shall especially renew our commitment to be companions of Jesus in his mission, committed as he is to the poor, committed to work with him in establishing his kingdom.[8]

The Society supposes that we are "men formed by the exercises" and genuinely tested by this foremost of our experiences, men who are continually renewing themselves in the dispositions of the Exercises. Different vocations each have their own respective charisms. For us nothing can replace the experience of the Exercises for maintaining both one's personal equilibrium and the unity of the Society. . . . If anyone after some years in the Society should doubt the truth of this, we would have to say either that he has not yet lived this unique experience or that he has failed in that test.[9]

3. *Life in Christ Jesus, Personal Love of Christ*

What is it to be Jesuit? It is to know that one is a sinner, yet called to be a companion of Jesus as Ignatius was: Ignatius, who begged the Blessed Virgin to "place him with her Son," and who then saw the Father himself ask Jesus, carrying his Cross, to take this pilgrim into his company.[10]

---

7 GC 31, D. 4, no. 2 [44].

8 GC 32, D. 4, no. 38 [87].

9 Father Arrupe, *ActRSJ*, XV, 29.

10 GC 32, D. 2, no. 1 [11], citing St. Ignatius' *Autobiography*, no. 96, found in MHSJ, *Fontes Narrativi*, I, 499. See also ibid., II, 133.

I. *The Fundamental Experience*

★

Behind the words, always approximations which can scarcely express the full reality, we must find the simple truth: Christ lives, speaks, and acts by receiving his being, his word, and his action from his Father. From Christ himself, too, does our own life flow forth and unfold, insofar as it too is a sharing in his relationships with his Father.[11]

★

Our aspiration is to proclaim the gospel in a personal love for the person of Jesus Christ, for an ever more inward knowledge of whom we daily ask, that we may the better love him and follow him; Jesus, whom we seek, as St. Ignatius sought, to experience; Jesus, Son of God, sent to serve, sent to set free, put to death, and risen from the dead. This love is the deepest well-spring of our action and our life.[12]

★

For the Jesuit, Christ is his example, his way, his life, and his strength—the poor Christ, the servant of his Father even to the sacrifice of himself. Therefore the Jesuit too wants to be stripped free of everything and emptied of himself, that he may find his security in God alone.[13]

4. *A Life Illumined by Faith*

In this "new age" . . . the Society of Jesus recognizes the difficulties with regard to its goal and plan of life which are arising from the changes that have taken place in man's way of living and thinking. . . . But all the members of the Society, firmly grounded in faith, in company with all other Christians, lift their eyes to Christ, in whom they find that absolute perfection of self-giving and undivided love which alone completely reconcile man to God and to himself. . . . Our Lord, with whose name our Society has been signed

---

11 Father Arrupe, *ActRSJ*, XV, 736.
12 GC 32, D. 2, nos. 26-27 [36-37].
13 Father Arrupe, *ActRSJ*, XV, 108.

and under the standard of whose cross it desires to serve the kingdom of his love, is himself the goal of human history, the point to which the desires of history and civilization converge, the center of the human race, the joy of all hearts and the fulfillment of all seeking.[14]

It is faith, constantly and progressively encompassing all human reality, that must permeate us as persons if we are to give authentic witness to the living presence of Christ the Lord.[15]

The Jesuit will see, with a deep faith, God's active presence and his plan of salvation in the aspirations, conflicts, and miseries of the human race in its present stage of development. He will recognize natural and human values, foster them in himself and others, raise them to a higher plane by consecrating them in their entirety to God, and guard himself against falling a victim to naturalism or letting his faith become weak and lifeless.

We are convinced that faith and the spirit of faith are a gift which we should beg with humility—"it will be given to you"—principally by prayer in which we renew our union with God in the midst of our work often done under pressure, and overcome by faith the temptations by which the world round about would seduce us.[16]

5. *"Magis," Abnegation, Humility*

Following St. Ignatius' methodology, "let us consider as addressed to ourselves" each of the great themes of the Spiritual Exercises, long familiar yet ever inexhaustible; for example, the dynamic power of that "magis" which excludes any form of mediocrity; that interior abnegation which is a condition for making a choice of what is better;

14 GC 31, D. 1, nos. 1, 6 [1, 14].
15 GC 31, D. 14, no. 3 [212].
16 Father Arrupe, *ActRSJ*, XV, 109.

the call of our Lord inviting us to be his friendship; God's will that we should love and serve him in all men and in all things, preferring those matters which advance us toward greater freedom from self-love.[17]

★

Our ambition is to proclaim the gospel in humility: realizing that there are many enterprises of great worth and moment in the Church and in the world which we, as priests and religious inspired by one particular charism, are not in a position to undertake. And even in those enterprises which we can and should undertake, we realize that we must be willing to work with others: with Christians, men of other religious faiths, and all men of good will; willing to play a subordinate, supporting, anonymous role; and willing to learn how to serve from those we seek to serve.

This availability for the meanest tasks, or at least the desire to be thus available, is part of the identity of the Jesuit. When he offers to distinguish himself in the service of the Eternal King, when he asks to be received under his standard, when he glories with Ignatius in being placed by the Father "with the Son," he does so not in any spirit of prideful privilege, but in the spirit of him who "emptied himself to assume the condition of a slave, even to accepting death, death on a cross."[18]

★

Deeply conscious of our utter unworthiness for so great a mission, relying only on God's love and grace, we offer together the prayer of Ignatius: "Take, O Lord, and receive, all my liberty; my memory, my understanding, and my entire will. Whatever I have or hold, you have given to me; I restore it all to you and surrender it wholly to be governed by your will. Give me only your love and your grace, and I am rich enough, and ask for nothing more."[19]

---

17 Father Arrupe, ibid., 29.
18 GC 32, D. 2, nos. 29-30 [39-40]; see also *SpEx,* [91, 147, 67]; *Autobiography,* no. 67; Phil. 2:7-8.
19 GC 32, D. 2, no. 32 [42]; *SpEx,* [234].

II. Spiritual Life, Life of Prayer

6. *"Spiritual" Life*

The spiritual life is participation in the life of the most holy Trinity dwelling within us so that we may be made conformed to the image of the Son of God, "so that he may be the firstborn among many brethren," for the glory of God.

This life involves the whole man and all his activities, by which he as a Christian corresponds to every impulse received from God. It does not consist only in individual acts of devotion, but ought to animate and direct our whole life, individual and community, together with all our relations to other persons and things. It is nourished and fostered by every grace by which God turns to us and communicates himself to us, especially by his word and the sacraments of Christ.

We for our part respond by the obedience of faith in which we give ourselves to God, "offering the full submission of intellect and will to God who reveals," celebrating as the high point of our life the sacred liturgy of the Lord's Eucharist, participating in the sacraments of Christ, and offering ourselves through love in all our actions, especially those which are apostolic, and all our hardships and joys.[20]

7. *The Union between Action and Prayer*

The Jesuit apostle . . . is a man called by his vocation to be "a contemplative in action". . . . Our intimate union with Christ forges a union of our life prayer of and our life of apostolic work. Far from living two separate lives, we are strengthened and guided towards action in our prayer while our action in turn urges us to pray. Bringing salvation to men in word and deed through faith, hope, and love, we pray as we work and are invited to formal prayer that we may toil as true servants of God. In this interplay, praise,

---

20 GC 31, D. 13, no. 5 [206-208]; see also Rom. 8:29; 16:26; Vat. II, on Revelation (DV), no. 5.

petition, thanksgiving, self-offering, spiritual joy, and peace join prayer and work to bring a fundamental unity into our lives.

Truly this is our characteristic way of prayer, experienced by St. Ignatius through God's special gift nourished by his own generous abnegation, fiery zeal for souls, and watchful care of his heart and senses. He found God in every thing, every word, and every deed. He relished God's omnipresence.[21]

8. *The Necessity of Prayer Itself*

We need personal prayer for the familiarity with God which consists in finding him in all things, and all things in him. Christ himself gave us an example of this. St. Ignatius urges it in both the Exercises and the Constitutions. Our own personal experience confirms it. For while it is "in action" that we are called to be contemplative, this cannot obscure the face that we *are* called to be "contemplative."[22]

Further, witness to Christ in our apostolate, we see him praying always to the Father, often alone through the night or in the desert. We, too, must enjoy familiar conversation with Him in continuous and formal prayer.[23]

A life consecrated to God, like apostolic dynamism itself, cannot produce its fruits or even endure unless God himself acts in us, and unless we on our part keep ourselves ever open to his action. St. Ignatius speaks often of this "being with Christ": "that [the Father] might place me with his Son," and that we might become "an instrument united with God". . . . In these matters we must linger on the words until we discover the undiminishable though hidden demands which they contain. "I have not yet won, but I am still running, trying to capture the prize for which Christ

21 GC 31, D. 14, no. 4 [213].
22 GC 32, D. 11, no. 8 [206].
23 GC 31, D. 14, no. 4 [213].

Jesus captured me";—"Your mind must be renewed by a spiritual revolution so that you can put on the new self."[24]

★

Prayer becomes not only a matter of obeying our religious rule, acceptable as that is to God, but also a personal reply to a divine call. Prayer is thus a faithful response to the law of charity towards God and men which the Holy Spirit has written in our hearts. For the charity of Christ itself urges us to personal prayer and no human person can dispense us from this urgency.[25]

9. *Praying by Inserting Oneself into the People of God, through the Sacraments and the Word of God*

Our life is inserted into that of the People of God, in which Christ shows us the way to the Father. Hence the prayer of every Christian is rooted in the prayer of the Church and flowers into liturgical action.[26]

★

Every Jesuit community is a faith community, and it is in the Eucharist that those who believe in Christ come together to celebrate their common faith. Our participation at the same table in the Body and Blood of Christ, more than anything else, makes us one companionship totally dedicated to Christ's mission in today's world.[27]

★

Since it has pleased the Father to speak to men both in his Son, the Word Incarnate, and in many ways in *Scripture,* the Bible, a treasure bestowed by the Spouse on his Church to nourish and guide all men, is truly an everflowing font of prayer and renewal of religious life. In each of us, as the whole tradition of the Church attests, Holy Scripture

---

24 Father Arrupe, *ActRSJ*, XV, 735; see also Phil. 3:12; Eph. 4:23-24; *Autobiography,* no. 96; *Cons,* [813].
25 GC 31, D. 14, no. 7 [218]; see also no. 11 [225-228]; GC 32, D. 11, no. 8 [206].
26 GC 31, D. 14, no. 5 [214].
27 GC 32, D. 11, no. 12 [210].

becomes our saving word only when heard in prayer that leads to the submission of faith. *Lectio divina,* a practice dating back to the earliest days of religious life in the Church, supposes that the reader surrenders to God who is speaking and granting him a change of heart under the action of the two-edged sword of Scripture continually challenging to conversion.[28]

10. *In Search of Familiarity with God through Personal Prayer*

In mental prayer we enjoy God's presence and action and try, with the aid of his grace, to see all things in the light of Christ. Through mental prayer our individual lives receive clarity and meaning from the history of salvation, are set against the background of God's speaking to us, and hopefully are enriched with that freedom and spiritual discernment so necessary for the ministry of the gospel. These reasons apply to all religious involved in the world of today, which far too often ignores its God. For these religious, formal prayer is a precious chance to see the unity of creation and to refer creation to the Father. Our own men, conscious of our special task of challenging atheism, find further apostolic significance in prayer as it fosters in us a sense of the living God and an encouragement of our faith.[29]

★

The Society counts on her men after their formation to be truly "spiritual men who have advanced in the way of Christ our Lord so as to run along this way," men who in this matter of prayer are led chiefly by that "rule . . . which discerning love gives to each one," guided by the advice of his spiritual father and the approval of his superior."[30]

★

All should recall that the prayer in which God communicates Himself more intimately is the better prayer,

---

28 GC 21, D. 14, no. 6 [215]; see also Vat. II, Revelation (DV), no. 25.
29 GC 31, D. 14, no. 3 [213].
30 GC 31, D. 14, no. 11 [228]; see also *Cons,* [582].

whether mental or even vocal, whether it be in meditative reading, or in an intense feeling of love and self-giving.[31]

★

And yet, many of us are troubled because, although we want to pray, we cannot pray as we would like and as our apostolic commitments demand we should. In the midst of our individual, isolated efforts to pray as we should, perhaps we should listen to Christ's reminder that "where two or three are gathered in my name, there am I in their midst." Does this not suggest that if we need assistance it is in our companionship that we must seek it: in dialogue with the spiritual counsellor, in openness to the superior, in shared prayer with our brothers?

Moreover, let us not forget that while our world poses obstacles in the way of our search for union with God in Christ, it also offers suggestions for surmounting those obstacles, which we should submit to an Ignatian discernment of spirits in order to determine where in them the Spirit of God is moving us. There is, for instance, the contemporary stress on spontaneous prayer, with a minimum of formalism. There is the interest in, and understanding of, the different approaches to union with God developed by the non-Christian religions. There are the various forms of prayer in community which lead to a mutually enriching exchange of faith experiences. There is, finally, the remarkable renewal taking place today in the giving and the making of the Spiritual Exercises, whose vivifying influence extends beyond the limits of the formal retreat into the daily life of prayer.[32]

11. *The Conditions of Prayer*

To live this life of prayer, which in the Society is never separated from apostolic action, each of us must first deny himself so that, shedding his own personal inclinations, he

---

31 GC 31, D. 14, no. 11 [228]; see also no. 7.

32 GC 32, D. 11, nos. 9-10 [207-208]; Matt. 18:20. See also footnote 8 on [208], where some examples are given.

may have that mind which is in Christ Jesus. For while, on the one hand, prayer brings forth abnegation, since it is God who purifies man's heart by his presence, on the other, abnegation itself prepares the way for prayer, because only the pure of heart will see God. Progress in prayer is possible for those alone who continually try to put off their misguided affections to ready themselves to receive the light and grace of God. This continual conversion of heart "to the love of the Father of mercies" is intimately related to the repeated sacramental act of penance.

Self-denial, which disposes us for prayer and is one of its fruits, is not genuine unless amid the confusion of the world we try to keep our hearts at peace, our minds tranquil, and our desires restrained.[33]

12. *Apostolic Action Based on Prayer Becomes Union with God*

Inwardly strengthened and renewed by prayer and the sacraments, we are able to make apostolic action itself a form of union with God. Our service of the faith [diakonia fidei] and our service of men then become, not an interruption of that union but a continuation of it, a joining of our action with Christ's salvific action in history. Thus contemplation flows into action regularly, and we realize to some extent our ideal of being contemplatives "in action."[34]

III. LIFE CONSECRATED BY THE THREE VOWS

13. *Consecration*

Inserted by baptism into the Mystical Body of Christ, strengthened by confirmation with the power of the Holy Spirit, and consecrated into a royal priesthood and a holy people, we receive a more special consecration for the divine service in the Society of Jesus by the profession of the evan-

---

33 GC 31, D. 14, no. 8 [219-220]; see also Vat. II, Priests (PO), no. 18.
34 GC 32, D. 11, no. 13 [211].

gelical counsels, so that we may be able to bring forth richer fruits from the grace of baptism.[35]

14. *Liberation*

If we commit ourselves until death to the evangelical counsels of poverty, chastity, and obedience, it is that we may be totally united to Christ and share his own freedom to be at the service of all who need us. In binding us, the vows set us free:

— free, by our vow of poverty, to share the life of the poor and to use whatever resources we may have not for our own security and comfort, but for service;

— free, by our vow of chastity, to be men for others, in friendship and communion with all, but especially with those who share our mission of service;

— free, by our vow of obedience, to respond to the call of Christ as made known to us by him whom the Spirit has placed over the Church, and to follow the lead of our superiors, especially our Father General, who has all authority over us *ad aedificationem*.[36]

15. *Prophetic Role*

It is in the light of the example of St. Ignatius and his first companions that we are asked to renew our dedication to the properly apostolic dimension of our religious life. Our consecration to God is really a prophetic rejection of those idols which the world is always tempted to adore: wealth, pleasure, prestige, power. Hence our poverty, chastity, and obedience ought visibly to bear witness to this. Despite the inadequacy of any attempt to anticipate the Kingdom which is to come, our vows ought to show how by God's grace there can be, as the gospel proclaims, a community among human beings which is based on sharing rather than on greed; on willing openness to all persons rather than on seeking after the privileges of caste or class or race; on ser-

---

35 GC 31, D. 13, no. 2 [203]; Vat. II, on the Laity (AA), no. 3.
36 GC 32, D. 2, no. 20 [3].

vice rather than on domination and exploitation. The men and women of our time need a hope which is eschatological, but they also need to have some signs that its realization has already begun.[37]

A. CHASTITY

16. *An Oblation to God*

Our vow of chastity consecrates a celibacy freely chosen for the sake of the Kingdom of God. By it, we offer an undivided heart to God, a heart capable of self-giving in service approaching the freedom from self-interest with which God himself loves all his creatures.[38]

17. *Its Apostolic Significance*

In the Society chastity too is essentially apostolic. It is not at all to be understood as directed exclusively to our personal sanctification. For, according to the whole intent of our Institute, we embrace chastity as a special source of spiritual fruitfulness in the world. Through it, full dominion of our energies, both bodily and spiritual, is retained for a prompter love and a more total apostolic availability towards all men. Moreover, the profession of chastity for the sake of the kingdom of heaven is of itself a true preaching of the gospel, for it reveals to all men how the kingdom of God prevails over every other earthly consideration, and it shows wonderfully at work in the Church the surpassing greatness of the force of Christ the King and the boundless power of the Holy Spirit.[39]

18. *Perfect Observance of Chastity*

God, pouring forth his charity in our hearts through the Holy Spirit, confers upon some in the Church the gift of

---

37 GC 32, D. 4, No. 16 [65]; John XXIII, *AAS,* 54 (1962), 682.
38 GC 32, D. 11, no. 26 [225]; see also GC 31, D. 16, nos. 3-4 [247-248].
39 GC 31, D. 16, no. 4 [248]; see also 1 Cor. 7:4; 7:32-33; Vat. II, on the Church (LG), nos. 42, 44; on Religious Life (PC), no. 12.

consecrated chastity, a sign of charity and likewise a stimulus to it, whereby they may more easily devote themselves with an undivided heart to him alone and to the service of his kingdom. Therefore, chastity "for the sake of the kingdom of heaven," to which by both his example and his calling Christ invites us, and which we as religious profess, following the lead of so many saints, should, as the Church repeatedly urges and as our founder expressly declares, be "perfectly observed" by us.[40]

19. *The Sacrifice Implied in Chastity and Its Fecundity*

On the other hand, chastity vowed to God through celibacy implies and requires of us a sacrifice by which we knowingly and willingly forego entrance into that family relationship wherein husband and wife, parents and children, can in many ways, even psychologically, attain mutual fulfilment. Hence, our consecration to Christ involves a certain affective renuntiation and a solitude of heart which form part of the cross offered to us by Jesus as we follow his footsteps, and closely associate us with his paschal mystery and render us sharers of the spiritual fertility which flows from it. The vow of chastity, then, on the indispensable condition that it be accepted with a humble, joyous, and firm spirit as a gift from God, and be offered as a sacrifice to God, not only does not diminish our personality nor hamper human contacts and dialogue, but rather expands affectivity, unites men fraternally, and brings them to a fuller charity.[41]

20. *The Necessity of Friendship with Christ and Familiarity with God*

All should cultivate close friendship with Christ and familiarity with God, for in the world, no one lives without love. But when our contemporaries question or fail to un-

---

40 GC 31, D. 16, no. 1 [245]; see also *Cons*, [547]; Matt. 19:11-12; 1 Cor. 7:7; Rom. 5:5; Vat. II, on the Church (LG), nos. 42, 46; Religious Life, no. 12.
41 GC 31, D. 16, no. 5 [249]; see also Vat. II, the Church (LG), no. 44; Priests (PO), no. 16; Priestly Formation (OT), no. 10.

derstand what our love is, we should offer them a fitting reply through the witness of a life of consecrated chastity, and at the same time with humble and persevering prayer we should beg for ourselves and our confreres the grace of personal love for Christ.

For our father Ignatius experienced this grace, so permeating his entire personality that he bound his brethren to himself as friends and by his personal affability led countless men and women to God.

In the Spiritual Exercises he wished to urge the imploring of this grace, so that throughout the meditations and contemplations on the mysteries of the life, death, and resurrection of our Lord Jesus Christ, and in the application of the senses to them he would have us beg to know interiorly the Lord "who for me was made man, so that I may love Him the more, and follow Him the more closely."[42]

21. *Constant Growth in Chastity*

Love consecrated by chastity should constantly grow and approach the mature measure of the fulness of Christ. It is, consequently, not a gift bestowed once and for all, mature and complete, at the beginning of one's spiritual life, but such as by repeated decisions, perhaps serious ones, should steadily increase and become more perfect. Thus the heart is more and more cleansed of affections not yet sufficiently understood, until the man adheres totally to Christ through love.[43]

22. *Friendship and Chastity*

Such love of Jesus our Lord impels a person likewise to genuine human love for men and to true friendship. For chastity for the sake of the kingdom of heaven is safeguarded by fraternal friendship and in turn flowers forth in it. Hence also, we should regard as the precious apostolic fruit of ever more perfect love of friendship that mature, simple, anxiety-free dealing with the men and women with whom and for

---

42 GC 31, D. 16, no. 8, a [252-254]; *SpEx,* [104].
43 GC 31, D. 16, no. 8, b [255].

whom we exercise our ministry for the building up of the body of Christ.

But to attain the perfect liberty of chaste love, besides the familiarity with God mentioned above, all the supernatural and natural helps available should be used.[44]

B. POVERTY

23. *Consecrated Poverty to Imitate Christ Poor and Humble*

Voluntary poverty in imitation of Christ is a sharing in that mystery revealed in the self-emptying of the very Son of God in the Incarnation. The Jesuit vocation to poverty draws its inspiration from the experience of St. Ignatius and the Spiritual Exercises and is specified by the Formula of the Institute and by the Constitutions. It is the charism of the Society to serve Christ poor and humble. The principle and foundation of our poverty, therefore, is found in a love of the Word made Flesh and crucified.[45]

Our first Fathers wanted to be "poor priests of Christ," not simply as a pastoral practice or exercise of philanthropy, but in order to respond to the call of the Father inviting them to attach themselves to Christ, to become like to him in a special way, and thus to take part in his salvific mission.[46]

Assuredly, we desire to bear witness, not to some ideology or virtue, but to Jesus Christ, and to the love and freedom he brings. . . . It is in the persons of those who voluntarily embrace poverty that "the poor of Yahweh"

44 GC 31, D. 16, no. 8, b, c [256-257]; see also Eph. 4:12; Vat. II, Priests (PO), nos. 11, 16; Religious Life (PC), no. 12.

45 GC 32, D. 12, no. 2 [258]; see also *SpEx,* [98, 147, 167]; Deliberation on Poverty, *Cons*MHSJ, I, 78-81; the Spiritual Diary of St. Ignatius, ibid., 86-158; FI, [5] (7); *Cons,* [553-581]; GC 31, D. 18, no. 3 [287].

46 Father Arrupe, *ActRSJ,* XV, 279; FI [5] (7).

may somehow live on. But above all, it is the Son of Man who lives in them, the Word of God born in the likeness of men. He, being found in the form of man, emptied himself and became humble, a servant, poor, hard-working, available to all, not claiming his own rights, and yet supremely free. . . .

Still further, when we contemplate the group of apostles living with Christ, and that community at Jerusalem animated by the Spirit of Christ given at Pentecost, we notice that power of charity which unites all those who desire to become brothers in Christ as well as witnesses to him. By that same dynamism of charity they are moved toward possessing all things in common and also toward sharing their material goods with all their brethren, so that all may be one: "Now the company of those who believed were of one heart and soul, and no one said that any of the things which he possessed was his own, but they had everything in common".[47]

24. *Apostolic Aspects*

Religious poverty still calls to the following of Christ poor, but also to a following of Christ at work in Nazareth, identifying with the needy in his public life, the Christ of heartfelt compassion, responding to their needs, eager to serve them.[48]

The Society cannot meet the demands of today's apostolate without reform of its practice of poverty. Jesuits will be unable to hear the "cry of the poor" unless they have greater personal experience of the miseries and distress of the poor. It will be difficult for the Society everywhere to forward effectively the cause of justice and human dignity if the greater part of her ministry identifies her with the rich and powerful, or is based on the "security of possession,

---

47 Father Arrupe, *ActRSJ*, XV, 277-278.
48 GC 32, D. 12, no. 4 [260]; see also no. 3; Paul VI, *Evangelica testificatio, AAS* (1971), nos. 17, 18, 20; Vat. II, the Church (LG), no. 44.

knowledge, and power." Our life will be no "witness to a new and eternal life won by Christ's redemption or to a resurrected state and the glory of the heavenly kingdom," if individually or corporately, Jesuits are seen to be attached to earthly things, even apostolic institutions, and to be dependent on them. Our communities will have no meaning or sign value for our times, unless by their sharing of themselves and all they possess, they are clearly seen to be communities of charity and of concern for each other and all others.[49]

★

Every Jesuit, no matter what his ministry, is called "to preach in poverty," according to the *sacra doctrina* of the Two Standards, and this poverty has a spiritual power not to be measured in human terms.

The faithful practice of religious poverty is apostolic, too, in its contempt of personal gain, which commends the gospel and frees the apostle to preach it in all its integrity. It is apostolic, finally, in that communities which are really poor, by their simplicity and fraternal union, proclaim the beatitudes, "manifesting to all believers the presence of heavenly goods already possessed here below."[50]

25. *An Essential Trait of Our Poverty: Life in Common without Having Anything of Our Own*

It is on the basis of our religious poverty as specially apostolic and because of the witness to truly liberal charity to which our vocation urges us, that we share in common not only our lives and our efforts, but also our material goods. Fraternal charity among apostles expresses itself particularly by this sharing and by the spontaneous care of equality as much as this is possible. . . .

---

49 GC 32, D. 12, no. 5 [261]; Ps. 9:13; Job 34:28; Prov. 12:13; Paul VII, *Evangelica testificatio, AAS* nos. (1971), 17, 19; Vat. II, the Church (LG), no. 44.

50 GC 32, D. 12, no. 9 [265]; see also *EppIgn*, I, 96; Vat. II, the Church (LG), no. 44; GC 31, D. 18, nos. 4, 7, 16, a [288, 291-292, 302]; D. 19, no. 7 [326 ff.]; Father Arrupe, *ActRSJ*, XV, 278.

III. *Life Consecrated by the Vows*

Common life demands a real bond, by which it becomes incarnate in the order of material things. For us this common life is not an end in itself; but it would no longer serve its purpose, fraternal and apostolic charity . . . , if an individualistic concept of the use of goods were allowed to prevail.

The authenticity of our apostolate cannot permit a return to private appropriation. On the contrary it requires, among other evidences, a sincere and efficacious willingness to an integral sharing of goods. The poor with whom our goods should be shared are first of all our brethren in the Society. For how can we make ourselves poor if we do not banish "mine and thine" from our fraternal life?

Assuredly times have changed and, for example, it is becoming increasingly accepted that many religious should have money on hand. Fidelity will consist now and in the future, not so much in asking permissions for small things (especially those virtually certain to be granted), but rather in a manner of acting characteristic of one who is not an owner but a member of a fraternal community, and therefore is acting according to the direction and intention of the Superior. Thus too the religious will spontaneously render an account of the money he has received and spent, and also submit his proposals in advance, for proper examination and approval.[51]

26. *Our Poverty Must Be Sincere*

Our profession of poverty should be sincere, so that the manner of our life corresponds to this profession. . . . The Society really intends to answer the demands of this real, not pretended poverty.[52]

Religious poverty should try hard to limit rather than to expand consumption. It is not possible to love poverty or experience its mysterious consolations, without some

51 Father Arrupe, *ActRSJ*, XV, 280-282.
52 GC 31, D. 18, no. 7 [291, 293]; GC 32, D. 12, no. 6 [262].

knowledge of its actuality. . . . The need for reform is so frequently evident and demanded by so many Provincial Congregations that no person or community may decline this examination.[53]

27. *Poverty, Work, Salary*

This witness of our poverty today most aptly shines forth in our practice and spirit of work undertaken for the kingdom of God and not for temporal gain. This poverty should be filled with activity, by which we resemble men who must earn their daily bread.[54]

Let us not say, however, that "For us, to be poor means to gain our living by means of our work," or that "each of us ought to provide for his own needs through renumeration from his personal work, or to bring some definite contribution to the house."

Manifestly, our spirit of poverty is not seriously carried into practice unless each one of us realistically and methodically employs his energies and time, even his liesure and holidays which law, scholastic ordinations, and other sources allow; and unless each one imposes on himself a life of dedicated work, reasonable hygiene or care of bodily health, and personal self-discipline. On all these the rich fruits of our energies are dependent. But the poverty of Christ and his disciples is lived out in any kind of activities, contemplative or intellectual, in ministries strictly spiritual as well as in other occupations necessary or useful—and that whether our service is an occasion of remuneration or gifts or whether nothing of this sort follows.[55]

We should not have any part in, or receive motivation from, that appetite for gain or hope of the delight which naturally accompanies an act of acquisition. We desired our

53 GC 32, D. 12, no. 7 [263].

54 GC 31, D. 18, no. 8 [294].

55 Father Arrupe, *ActRSJ,* XV, 283-284.

lives to be freed from desire for gain, often a tyrannical force. Does not the modern world have need of men who boldly bear witness to this liberation? A responsibility far more urgent than that of earning sustenance should impel us, namely, our apostolic responsibility. We accept the risks entailed by an indifference toward gain, so that, in whatever place God wills, we may serve and love with full liberty and availability. For what else does Ignatian gratuity mean? . . . The authenticity of our apostolate would perish if Jesuits were to acquire for themselves the fruit of their labor, or if they were to accept or reject ministries insofar as they could or could not garner a large stipend, or if Superiors in undertaking apostolic enterprises or in assigning work and places to Jesuits were to let themselves be led by a concern for financial gain.[56]

28. *Jesuit Poverty and Insecurity*

We have no lack of vivid experience of what the giving up of security means if we follow common life in the full meaning of the term. If some Jesuit as a matter of fact does receive considerable revenues from the services he renders and hands them over in their entirety to the community; or if a Jesuit before his last vows renounces his inheritance in favor of works in the administration of which he will have no voice; or if some formed Jesuit, upon whom by civil law an ample inheritance devolves, in regard to which he is not to make any determination—do not these Jesuits experience the true meaning of insecurity, and also the joy of a risk generously embraced and not merely tolerated in passive manner? . . .

From another viewpoint, however, evangelical and religious poverty cannot be reduced simply to deprivation of security, nor is this security itself confined to the economic sphere. Our very norm of community of goods, which norm should of course be so adapted that its practice in fact corresponds to modern times and circumstances, makes real and profound demands upon us. Assuredly this common life

---

56 Father Arrupe, ibid., 288.

includes the mark of dependence and, if we look deeper, of humility. Those who know poor wage-earners more intimately, and those who have examined the condition of poor nations or classes, observe that the heaviest burden oppressing such people is their condition of subjection and humiliation. Among workers, those are deemed poorest who are not free to choose their work, its place or time, their foremen or fellow workers, and also those who are forced to emigrate from their native country. . . . Therefore, even in regard to our being made like the humble and weak of the modern world, we perceive how important is the life of dependence which springs from our common life and our vow of poverty. This dependence has nothing ignoble about it. Rather, it is something noble, insofar as we have freely chosen this obligation, inspired by our love of Christ, the humiliated servant, and have thus been made sharers of that love for his least ones which springs from his Heart.[57]

No one can fail to observe that our poverty, determined by definite institutional structures, is exposed to the danger of formalism (having, for example, a dependence merely fictitious). But it should be noticed that such a danger is common to any profession of poverty. Whether there is an institution or not, if those who make profession of being witnesses to a higher manner of living will at some time or other enter into easier ways, they will always fall into some type of pharisaism or of other scandal. The fact is, however, that the charism of any religious society develops a need for an institution and creates one in which it can take on flesh and bones and pass into the realm of concrete existence.[58]

29. *Poverty and Sharing; Service of the Poor*

Our poverty should become a sign of our charity in that by our lack we enrich others. Nothing should be our own so that all things may be common in Christ. Communities

---

57 Father Arrupe, ibid., 290-291.
58 Father Arrupe, ibid., 293. (The first words are adapted from p. 292.)

themselves, renouncing their own advantage, should be united to each other by the bond of solidarity. Finally, the parts of the Society should freely become poorer so that they may serve the whole body of the Society. And the bond of charity should not be restricted only to Jesuits, for all men are related to the Mystical Body of Christ. Charity should always crown the obligations of justice by which we are bound in a special way to those who are poorer and to the common good.[59]

★

The Society, facing a world in which a large part of mankind lies wounded and despoiled, moved by the love of the Good Samaritan, and conscious of its universal vocation, should subject its apostolate to examination, to see how it may more fully turn itself to those who are abandoned, "to evangelize the poor, to heal the crushed in heart."[60]

The Church regards the ministry of promotion of justice as integral to the contemporary practice of poverty. Such commitment is everywhere needed, but in many places it is a very condition of credibility for the Society and for the Church. The insertion of communities among the poor so that Jesuits may work for them and with them, or at least may acquire some experience of their condition, is a testimony of the love of the poor and of poverty to which the Church encourages religious.[61]

30. *Interior Disposition and Effective Experience*

All should remember that no community form of poverty nor any outward profession of it will be genuinely Christian unless it is inspired by a highly personal sentiment of the heart, that is, by a spiritual poverty, drawn from a close and constant union with the Incarnate Word of God. Therefore,

---

59 GC 31, D. 18, no. 9 [295]; see also no. 8 [294].

60 GC 31, D. 18, no. 11 [297]; Luke 4:18; *SpEx*, [167].

61 GC 32, D. 12, no. 10 [266]; see also Paul VI, *Evangelica testificatio, AAS* (1971), nos. 18, 20; *Cons*, [580]; *GenExam*, [81].

there is a broad field of personal responsibility in which each can more perfectly live his calling to poverty and, within the limits of the common good, express it with discerning love by living more frugally, under the guidance of superiors.[62]

★

Evangelical poverty is a mystery for the human mind, and reason alone is not able to explain or hold it up as good. There is only one means for a man to grasp the meaning and riches of this mystery: a genuine experience of poverty in the concrete. The simple desire to be poor does not suffice. To acquire a true acceptance of poverty with our affections, we must experience its effects. How shall we genuinely love and desire poverty unless we have known it through experience? When we shall experience real poverty, we shall also experience its marvelous fruits in abundance. For one who embraces it lovingly often experiences a joy, happiness, and inner freedom such, he admits, as he had never felt before.[63]

C. OBEDIENCE

31. *Mission and Obedience*

Impelled by love of Christ, we embrace obedience as a distinctive grace conferred by God on the Society through its founder, whereby we may be united the more surely and constantly with God's salvific will, and at the same time he made one in Christ among ourselves. For the Society of Jesus is a group of men who seek close union with Christ and a share in the saving mission which he realized through obedience unto death. Christ invited us to take part in such a mission when, bearing his cross, he told St. Ignatius at La Storta, "I will that you serve us." Through obedience, then, strengthened by vow, we follow "Jesus Christ still carrying

---

62 GC 31, D. 18, no. 10 [296]. See also *Cons,* [580]; FI, [5] (8).

63 Father Arrupe, letter to a certain Provincial's inquiry on Poverty, Old Goa, India, January 8, 1973.

his cross in the Church militant, to whom the eternal Father gave us as servants and friends, that we may follow him with our cross" and be made his companions in glory. . . . Now through the vow of obedience our Society becomes a more fit instrument of Christ in his Church, unto the assistance of souls for God's greater glory.[64]

★

A Jesuit, therefore, is essentially a man on a mission: a mission which he receives immediately from the Holy Father and from his own religious superiors, but ultimately from Christ himself, the one sent by the Father. It is by being sent that the Jesuit becomes a "companion of Jesus."[65]

32. *Obeying the Superior for the Love of Christ*

The first Fathers of the Society held the unshaken conviction that "they had no other head than Christ Jesus, whom alone they hoped to serve," and they solemnly sanctioned this fact in the Formula of the Institute, affirming that they wanted "to serve the Lord alone." In the same Formula, however, they already expressly declared that "they are serving the Lord alone and the Church his spouse, under the Roman pontiff," understanding that they offer obedience to Christ himself when they obey the visible head of the Church. Moreover, in the deliberation of the first Fathers, all decided unanimously that they should obey not only the Vicar of Christ, but also the superior chosen from among them, "so that we can more sincerely and with greater praise and merit fulfil through all things the will of God." St. Ignatius repeatedly states this, that every superior is to be obeyed "in the place of Christ and for the love of Christ."[66]

★

---

64 GC 31, D. 17, no. 2. See also Vat. II, Religious life (PC), no. 14; in MHSJ, *Monumenta Nadal,* IV, 678; V, 296.

65 GC 32, D. 2, no. 14 [24]. See also John 17:18; GC 32, D. 4, nos. 66, 69 [114, 118].

66 GC 31, D. 17, no. 3 [270], citing Polanco, *Fontes narrativi,* I, 204; FI, [3] (1); Deliberation of the First Fathers in *Cons*MHSJ, I, 4; *GenExam,* [83, 85]; *Cons,* [286, 424, 547, 551].

Just as the Son of God "emptied himself, taking the form of a servant, being born in the likeness of men"; just as He "humbled himself and became obedient unto death, even death on a cross," so also do members of the Society from love for Christ and to gain souls, "offer the full dedication of their own will as a sacrifice of self to God." Thus they bind themselves entirely to God, beloved above all, and by a new and special title dedicate and consecrate themselves to his service and honor, bearing witness to the new freedom whereby Christ has made us free.[67]

33. *Obedience Full and Sincere*

Hence, not just any sort of obedience is expected of us, but an obedience full and generous, of the intellect, too, insofar as possible, rendered in a spirit of faith, humility, and modesty.

Our holy father St. Ignatius desired that we should all excel in the virtue of obedience. Accordingly, with all our force and energy we should strive to obey, first, the Sovereign Pontiff, and then the superiors of the Society, "not only in matters of obligation, but also in others, even at the mere hint of the superior's will, apart from any express command." We are to respond with perfect obedience in all things where there is not manifestly any sin.[68]

34. *The Obligation of Responsibility*

Obedience is the ordinary means by which God's will is made clear to the members of the Society. However, it does not take away, but rather by its very nature and perfection supposes in the subject the obligation of personal responsibility and the spirit of ever seeking what is better. Consequently the subject can, and sometimes should, set forth his own reasons and proposals to the superior. Such a way of acting is not opposed to perfect obedience, but is reasonably

---

67 GC 31, D. 17, no. 12 [281]; Phil. 2:7-8; Vat. II, Religious Life (PC), no. 14.

68 GC 31, D. 17, nos. 9, 10 [277-287]. See also *Cons,* [284, 547, 549]; St. Ignatius, *Letter on Obedience,* nos. 2, 3.

required by it, in order that by an effort common to both superior and subject the divine will may more easily and surely be found.[69]

35. *Meaning of "Obedience of Judgment"*

For obedience of judgment does not mean that our intellect is bereft of its proper role, and that one should assent to the superior's will against reason, rejecting the evidence of truth. For the Jesuit, employing his own intelligence, confirmed by the unction of the Holy Spirit, makes his own the will and judgment of superiors, and with his intellect endeavors to see their orders as more conformed to the will of God. He diverts his attention from a fretful consideration of the opposite reasons, and directs it solely to positive reasons intrinsic to the matter or to motives which transcend this order, namely, values of faith and charity. For practical matters are at issue, in which almost always there remains some doubt as to what is most fitting and more pleasing to God. Theoretical certitude or very high probability about the objective superiority of a given solution is not to be awaited before a superior can authoritatively impose it; nor are the reasons for a course of action always and everywhere to be given the subject that he may devote himself wholeheartedly to the goals and works assigned to him. For the final reason for religious obedience is the authority of the superior. Trust is to be placed in Christ, who by means of obedience wishes to lead the Church and the Society to the ends he proposes.[70]

36. *Spiritual Government*

After the example of Christ, whose place he holds, the superior should exercise his authority in a spirit of service, desiring not to be ministered unto, but to serve. . . . While he maintains sincere interior reverence, he should exercise

---

69 GC 31, D. 17, no. 11 [280]. See also Vat. II, Priests (PO), no. 15; *GenExam,* [92, 131]; *Cons,* [292, 543, 627].

70 GC 31, D. 17, no. 11 [280]; see also *Cons,* [284, 550, 619]; GC 32, D. 11, no. 31 [231].

simplicity in his way of speaking, so that the friendly con-
cord of Christ with his apostles may come to view. . . .

Hence government in the Society should always be
spiritual, conscious before God of personal responsibility
and of the obligation to rule one's subjects as sons of God
and with regard for the human personality, strong where it
needs to be, open and sincere. . . .

In the exercise of authority, however, the gift of discretion
or of discerning love is most desirable. To acquire this virtue, so necessary for good government, the superior should
first of all be free from ill-ordered affections and be closely
united and familiar with God. . . . Besides, he ought to
know thoroughly our ways of acting, according to our
Institute. Keeping in view, then, our end, which is none
other than the greater service of God and the good of those
who engage in this course of life, he should command the
things which he believes will contribute towards attaining
the end proposed by God and the Society, maintaining
withal due respect for persons, places, times, and other circumstances.[71]

37. *Familiar Exchange between Superior and Com-panions; Account of Conscience*

The communication between the superior and his
brothers should be, as far as possible, plain and open. The
superior should endeavor to make his mind clearly known
to his confreres and understood by them; and he should take
care that they, according to the nature and importance of
the matter and as their own talents and duties require,
share more fully in his knowledge and concern both for the
personal and community life of Jesuits and for their
apostolic labors. The religious, for his part, should try to
make himself known, with his gifts and limitations, his
desires, difficulties, and ideas, through a continuing, confiding, familiar, and candid colloquy, about which the
superior is held to strict secrecy. In this way an account of

---

71 GC 31, D. 17, nos. 4-5 [271-272]; see also FI, [4] (6); *Cons,* [161, 219, 222, 423, 624, 723, 726, 729, 746].

conscience is obtained which is sincere and open in form, and not reduced to a formal, periodic inquiry about actions already performed. That kind of a friendly and confidential conversation, one that is frankly spiritual and aims at promoting the apostolic objective of our vocation and the religious sanctification of the apostle, will constitute the dialogue that is fundamental and essential for the wholesome progress of our Society. Hence it is the mind of the Congregation that the account of conscience in its proper sense should remain and be strengthened as a general practice. But it is charity that should inspire it, as St. Ignatius wished, with any obligation under pain of sin always precluded.[72]

The contemporary stress on individual initiative, combined with the wide range of opportunities open to that initiative, tends to obscure the sense of mission essential to Ignatian obedience and may dislodge it altogether, unless we make fuller use of the special instrument for spiritual governance bequeathed to us by St. Ignatius: the *account of conscience.* . . .

Both the superior who sends and the companion who is sent gain assurance that the mission is really God's will if it is preceded by the dialogue that is the account of conscience.[73]

38. *Consultation with Many, or Even All*

But in order that he may more easily discover the will of God, the superior should have at hand able advisers and should often consult them. He should also use the services of experts in reaching decisions on complex matters. This will the more easily enable members of the Society to be convinced that their superior knows how, wants, and is able, to govern them well in the Lord. Besides, since all who work together in God's service are under the influence of the Holy

---

72 GC 31, D. 17, no. 8 [275]; *Cons,* [551].
73 GC 32, D. 11, nos. 30-31 [230-231].

Spirit and his grace, it will be well in the Lord to use their ideas and advice so as to understand God's will better.

Superiors in the Society should readily and often ask for and listen to the counsel of their brethren, of a few or of many, or even of all gathered together, according to the importance and nature of the matter.[74]

39. *The Superior's Role in Community Discernment*

What is the role of the superior in communitarian discernment? It is, first, to develop, as far as he can, the requisite disposition for it; second, to decide when to convoke the community for it, and clearly to define its object; third, to take active part in it as the bond of union within the community and as the link between the community and the Society as a whole; and, finally, to make the final decision in the light of the discernment, but freely, as the one to whom both the grace and the burden of authority is given. For in our Society the discerning community is not a deliberative or capitular body but a consultative one, whose object, clearly understood and fully accepted, is to assist the superior to determine what course of action is for God's greater glory and the service of men.[75]

40. *Subsidiarity and the Superior's Trust in His Companions*

It is also advantageous to the Society that the superior leave much in his orders to the prudence of his confreres, making liberal use of the principle of subsidiarity. To the extent that they make the spirit of the Society their own, especially if they are men long proven in humility and self-denial, individuals are to be allowed suitable freedom in the Lord. And finally, the universal good itself will sometimes demand that, in the manner of urging what has been commanded, account be taken also of human frailty.[76]

---

74 GC 31, D. 17, no. 6[273]; *Cons*, [667; see also 221, 810]; *Determinaciones antiguas,* no. 45, in *Cons*MHSJ, 218-219; Vat. II, Religious Life (PC), no. 14.

75 GC 32, D. 11, no. 24 [222].

76 GC 31, D. 17, no. 7 [274].

IV. UNION AND COMMUNITY

41. *Union and Community; Values of Apostolic Life*

It is in companionship that the Jesuit fulfils his mission. He belongs to a community of friends in the Lord who, like him, have asked to be received under the standard of Christ the King.[77]

The sense of community evolved gradually in the infant Society. The first members, "friends in the Lord," after they had offered themselves and their lives to Christ the Lord and given themselves to his Vicar on earth that he might send them where they could bear more fruit, decided to associate themselves into one body so that they might make stronger and more stable every day their union and association which was begun by God, "making ourselves into one body, caring for and understanding one another for the greater good of souls."[78]

The dispersal imposed on us today by our vocation as Jesuits makes it imperative that we strengthen and renew the ties that bind us together as members of the same Society. That is why it is so important that our communities be apostolic communities, and it is the primary responsibility of the local superior to see to it that his community approach this ideal as closely as possible. Each one of us should be able to find in his community—in shared prayer, in converse with his brethren, in the celebration of the Eucharist—the spiritual resources he needs for the apostolate. The community should also be able to provide him with a context favorable to apostolic discernment.[79]

---

77 GC 32, D. 2, no. 15 [25].

78 GC 31, D. 19, no. 1 [312], citing Ignatius to Verdolay, July 24, 1537, in *EppIgn,* I, 119; see also Favre, letter to de Gouvea, Nov. 23, 1538, *EppIgn,* I, 132; *Cons,* [605]; Deliberation of the First Fathers, *Cons*MHSJ, I, 3.

79 GC 32, D. 4, nos. 62-63 [111-112].

The Jesuit community is also a community of discernment. The missions on which Jesuits are sent, whether corporately or individually, do not exempt us from the need of discerning together in what manner and by what means such missions are to be accomplished.[80]

The Society does not consist of a group of men merely living side by side who look for certain advantages from their association more or less structured, with each one exercising an apostolate on his own. Rather, the Society is genuinely an apostolic body, essentially one, possessing its own peculiar and dynamic unity, and built up out of the very variety of its tasks into a kind of organic whole by means of a bond of wills, through the joints and sinews of obedience.[81]

Community life is not for us a goal to be sought for its own sake. Rather, the term or center upon which the apostolic activities of all our members converge is usually outside the circle of that community life taken in its material sense, and is found in those whom we serve. This, as you readily see, is the true reason why a communitarian character should stamp the entire apostolate of the Society. This stamp or element of our activity should be safeguarded and aimed at by the life inside the community circle itself, the community life in its stricter sense.[82]

Hence, what St. Ignatius says about the need for union of minds and hearts among us was never more true than now: "The more difficult it is for members of this congregation to be united with their head and among themselves, since they are so scattered among the faithful and among unbelievers in diverse regions of the world, the more ought

---

80 GC 32, D. 2, no. 19 [29].

81 Father Arrupe, *ActRSJ,* XV, 118.

82 Father Arrupe, ibid.

means to be sought for that union. For the Society cannot be preserved, or governed, or, consequently, attain the end it seeks for the greater glory of God, unless its members are united among themselves and with their head."[83]

42. *Our Community Is the Local Community, the Province, and the Whole Body of the Society*

Our community is the entire body of the Society itself, no matter how widely dispersed over the face of the earth. The particular local community to which one may belong at any given moment is, for him, simply a concrete—if, here and now, a privileged—expression of this world-wide brotherhood.[84]

★

The apostolic body of the Society to which we belong should not be thought of just in terms of the local community. We belong to a province, which should itself constitute an apostolic community in which discernment and coordination of the apostolate on a larger scale than at the local level can and should take place. Moreover, the province is part of the whole Society, which also forms one single apostolic body and community. It is at this level that the overall apostolic choices and guidelines must be decided and worked out, choices and guidelines for which we should all feel jointly responsible.[85]

43. *A Community Which Is Religious Properly so Called*

In the Society of Jesus, community takes its origin from the will of the Father joining us into one, and is constituted by the active, personal, united striving of all members to fulfill the divine will, with the Holy Spirit impelling and guiding us individually through responsible obedience to a life which is apostolic in many ways. It is a community of

---

83 GC 32, D. 11, no. 4 [202; *Cons,* [655].

84 GC 32, D. 2, no. 16 [26].

85 GC 32, D. 4, no. 68 [117].

men who are called byChrist to live withChrist, to be conformed to Christ, to fulfill the work of Christ in themselves and among men.[86]

By forming in this way a community of brothers, we bear witness to the presence of God among men: God who, as Trinity, is, beyond all imagining, a community of Love; God who, made man, established with men an everlasting covenant.[87]

44. *Conditions of Union in the Body of the Society and in Our Communities*

Where, then, do we begin in our efforts to foster union in the Society and in our communities? We begin with the Ignatian insight that the unity of an apostolic body such as ours must be based on the close union of each and all with God in Christ. For if we have come together as a companionship, it is because we have, each of us, responded to the call of Christ the Eternal King.[88]

The union of minds of the members among themselves and with their head, leading to personal holiness and at the same time to apostolic activity, flows from a love for our God and Lord, Jesus Christ, and is sustained and governed by the same love.[89]

This union of minds will be effected mainly by "the bond of obedience, which unites individuals with their superiors, and these among themselves and with the provincials, and all with Father General."[90]

---

86 GC 31, D. 19, no. 2 [313]; see also GC 32, D. 11, no. 14 [212].
87 GC 32, D. 11, no. 15 [213]; John 13:34-35.
88 GC 32, D. 11, no. 6 [204]; *Cons,* [655-671].
89 GC 31, D. 19, no. 3 [314].
90 GC 31, D. 17, no. 13 [282]; *Cons,* [821].

45. *Our Community Is also a Fraternal Union, Koinonia*

Our community is "a community in view of dispersion," but also a *koinonia,* a sharing of goods and life, with the Eucharist at its center: the sacrifice and sacrament of the Deed of Jesus, who loved his own to end. And each member of every Jesuit community is ever mindful of what St. Ignatius says about love, that it consists in sharing what one has, what one is, with those one loves. When we speak of having all things in common, that is what we mean.[91]

By this love, which contains a real offering of one's self to others, a true brotherhood in the Lord is formed, which constantly finds human expression in personal relationships and mutual regard, service, trust, counsel, edification, and encouragement of every kind.[92]

However, the analogy of family life cannot be applied to our apostolic friendship in the Lord without certain qualifications. . . . The attempt to regard our community life as similar to the ideal of family life might square more with a fictitious ideal than with reality, and might result in deceiving our members, who would thus be led along a path foreign to the meaning of their vocation. If at times we experience, in spite of the atmosphere of reciprocal charity, a certain psychological austerity, do we not then really feel that sacrifice we made in renouncing both the founding of a family and the right to the free and enjoyable use of our leisure, in order to devote our whole hearts and all our time to the Lord and to men?[93]

46. *Communication in Our Community Life*

For fostering our community life great importance should be given to every kind of exchange of information in the

---

91 GC 32, D. 2, no. 18 [28]; John 13:1; *SpEx,* [231].
92 GC 31, D. 19, no. 5, a [317].
93 Father Arrupe, *ActRSJ,* XV, 119.

community, . . . consultation, . . . delegation, . . . and collaboration transcending every sort of individualism. . . . In our communities, too, a style of life should be established, flexible but also firm, which favors personal and community prayer, promotes individual and communitarian work, makes mutual interchange among the members easier, provides for the relaxation of tensions and the celebration of life, and, finally, establishes a climate in which men dedicated to apostolic service can—as the apostles of Jesus did—grow to the height of their vocation.[94]

Fraternal communication within the community can take many forms according to different needs and circumstances. But its basic presupposition is, at the human level, sincerity and mutual trust and, at the level of grace, those gifts of God with which our companionship began and by which it is maintained.[95]

Certain features of our Ignatian heritage can be given a communitarian dimension; provided, of course, the personal practice for which they were originally intended in not abandoned. For instance, the examination of conscience could, at times, be made a shared reflection on the community's fidelity to its apostolic mission. Similarly, fraternal correction and personal dialogue with the superior can usefully become a community review of community life style.[96]

We can go further and say that community spiritual interchange can, under certain conditions, become *communitarian discernment*. This is something quite distinct

---

94 GC 31, D. 19, no. 5, b-f [318-322] (summarized here); also GC 32, D. 11, no. 18 [216]; Mark 6:30-31.

95 GC 32, D. 11, no. 19 [217]; see also *Cons,* [134, 812]; Father Arrupe, *ActRSJ,* XV, 123-124.

96 GC 32, D. 11, no. 20 [218].

from the usual community dialogue. It is "a corporate search for the will of God by means of a shared reflection on the signs which point where the Spirit of Christ is leading," and the method to follow in such communitarian discernment is analogous to that which St. Ignatius teaches for the making of a personal decision on a matter of importance.

There are prerequisites for a valid communitarian discernment. On the part of the individual member of the community, a certain familiarity with the Ignatian rules for the discernment of spirits, derived from actual use; a determined resolution to find the will of God for the community whatever it may cost; and, in general, the dispositions of mind and heart called for and cultivated in the First and Second Weeks of the Exercises. On the part of the community as such, a clear definition of the matter to be discerned, sufficient information regarding it, and "a capacity to convey to one another what each one really thinks and feels."[97]

This type of community interchange demands the degree of maturity, integration, and balance necessary to overcome any inhibitions and tensions, and to clear the way to a frank and open communication of each one's personal opinions and trends of thought. Such community interchange somehow presupposes, or at the same time helps to create, a community habituated to examining itself in regard to its apostolate, its daily life, and the various habits and attitudes of its members. . . . In a community constituted thus, it is not difficult to make the transition from the level of reasoning properly so called and of weighing reasons to the level of spiritual perception of the will of God in regard to daily life as concretely lived, and also in the various problems brought under consideration. All this is indeed an extension and further application of St. Ignatius' spiritual methodology; and in it the communitarian dimension ought

---

97 GC 32, D. 11, nos. 21-22 [219-220]; see also Father Arrupe, *ActRSJ*, XV, 769; *SpEx*, [169-189].

not in any way to lessen, but rather to reinforce, the fidelity which each of us should render to the Holy Spirit.[98]

★

This communal search for God's will through spiritual discernment is carried out according to the mind of the Society by means of dialogue whenever we look for signs of the operation of the Spirit of Christ, in order to know what holiness requires of us, and in order that the community, going forward continually in the spirit of the gospel, may thereby become more apostolic.[99]

47. *Communion in Thinking and Feeling with the Church*

Our being united among ourselves depends, in the last analysis, on our being united in both mind and heart to the Church that Christ founded. The historical context in which Saint Ignatius wrote his Rules for Thinking with the Church is, of course, different from ours. But there remains for us the one pillar and ground of truth, the Church of the living God, in which we are united by one faith and one baptism to the one Lord and the Father. It behooves us, then, to keep undimmed the spirit of the Ignatian rules and apply them with vigor to the changed conditions of our times.[100]

48. *Facing Today's Difficulties*

But let us realistically face the facts that make community building difficult today. More so today than in the past, our membership is drawn from very different social and cultural backgrounds. Moreover, the modern world places a much heavier stress on individual freedom than on the subordination of the individual to the group. Our response to these realities will be to transform them from obstacles to aids in community building. Our basic attitude towards cultural differences will be that they can enrich our union rather

---

98 Father Arrupe, *ActRSJ,* XV, 769.
99. Father Arrupe, ibid., XV, 123.
100 GC 32, D. 11, no. 33 [233]; 1 Tim. 3:15; Eph. 4:5.

than threaten it. Our basic attitude towards personal freedom will be that freedom is fulfilled in the active service of love.

Not that we should adopt an attitude of indiscriminate tolerance, a weary attitude of "peace at any price." Our attitude should be, rather, that of the Contemplation for Obtaining Love: "to consider how all blessings and gifts descend from above, such as my limited power from the supreme and limitless Power on high, and so with justice, goodness, piety, mercy; as rays from the sun, as water from the spring." We come to the Society from many lands, many ways of thought and life, each one of which has received a particular grace from God's infinite bounty. As companions of Jesus and each other, we wish to share with one another what we have and are, for the building up of communities dedicated to the apostolate of reconciliation.[101]

★

Times of stress and trial that might threaten our fraternal communion from time to time can become moments of grace, which confirm our dedication to Christ and make that dedication credible.[102]

49. *Community Life Strengthens Religious Life*

When community life flourishes, the whole religious life is sound. Obedience, for instance, is a very clear expression of our cooperation toward common ends, and it becomes more perfect to the extent that superiors and subjects are bound to one another in trust and service. Chastity is more safely preserved, "when there is a true brotherly love in community life between the members." Poverty, finally, means that we have made ourselves poor by surrendering ourselves and our possessions to follow the Lord. Community life aids and assists us in this surrender in a great variety of ways, and in its own unique way is the support of poverty. When the religious life is thus strengthened, unity

---

101 GC 32, D. 11, nos. 16-17 [214-215]; *SpEx,* [237].
102 GC 32, D. 11, no. 25 [223].

and flexibility, universality, full personal dedication, and evangelical freedom, are also strengthened for the assistance of souls in every way. And this was the intention of the first companions.

In addition, community life itself is a manifold testimony for our contemporaries, especially since by it brotherly love and unity are fostered, by which all will know that we are disciples of Christ.[103]

Clearly, the union of minds and hearts of which we speak is difficult of achievement. Equally clearly, it is demanded by our apostolic mission. Our witness to the gospel would not be credible without it. The sincere acceptance and willing execution of these orientations and norms set forth by this present Congregation will help towards that union. But human means fall short. It is the Spirit of God, the Spirit of love, that must fill the Society. For this we humbly pray.[104]

V. CONSTANT SPIRITUAL RENEWAL, PERMANENT FORMATION

50. *Spiritual Life Should Be Ever Renewed*

Closely following the Church, which, in liturgical renewal, biblical and theological reflection, and attention to the changing conditions of the times, is led by the Holy Spirit to complement the wisdom of antiquity by means of new developments, all, even those who have already completed their formation, should strive constantly to draw from these sources renewal for their own spiritual lives. Their apostolic activity will thus be enabled to answer more effectively the needs of the Church and of men.[105]

51. *The Life of Study Never Ends*

Our apostolic calling requires personal and ever-

---

103 GC 31, D. 19, no. 4 [315]; John 13:35; Vat. II, Religious Life (PC), no. 15.
104 GC 32, D. 11, no. 34 [234].
105 GC 31, D. 8, no. 46 [138].

deepening study not only on the part of the young but on the part of all Jesuits. . . .

Especially in our times, when everything is subject to such rapid change and evolution, and when new questions and new knowledge, both in theology and in other branches of learning, are constantly developing, a truly contemporary apostolate demands of us a process of permanent and continuing formation. Thus formation is never ended, and our "first" formation must be seen as the beginning of this continuing process. . . .

Continuing formation is achieved especially through a constant evaluation of and reflection on one's apostolate, in the light of faith and with the help of one's apostolic community. It also needs the cooperation of our professors and experts, whose theory can shed light on our praxis, even while they themselves are led to more profound reflection by the apostolic experience of their fellow Jesuits. This kind of communication will also assist the integration of the young into the apostolic life of the province, and the contact between formation and the apostolate will profit the whole Society.[106]

---

106 GC 32, D. 6, nos. 4, 18, 19 [136, 150, 151].

PART II

NORMS AND PRACTICAL DIRECTIVES

SACRAMENTAL AND PERSONAL PRAYER

1. Because "the work of our redemption is constantly carried on in the mystery of the Eucharistic Sacrifice," all of our members should consider daily celebration of the Eucharist as the center of their religious and apostolic life. Concelebrations are encouraged, especially on days when the community can more easily gather together.[1]

2. In reciting the Divine Office, our priests should try to pray attentively and at a suitable time that wonderful song of praise which is truly the prayer of Christ and that of his Body to the Father.[2]

3. In order to respond to the interior need for familiarity with God, we should all spend some time each day in personal prayer. Therefore, for those still in formation, "the Society retains the practice of an hour and a half as the time for prayer, Mass, and thanksgiving. Each man should be guided by his spiritual father as he seeks that form of prayer in which he can best advance in the Lord. The judgment of superiors is normative for each."

For others, "our rule of an hour's prayer is to be adapted so that each Jesuit, guided by his superiors, takes into ac-

---

1 GC 32, D. 11, no. 35 [235]; Vat. II, Priests (PO), no. 13; see also GC 31, D. 14, no. 10 [224].
2 GC 31, D. 14, no. 10 [224]; Vat. II, Priests (PO), no. 5; Liturgy (SC), nos. 84, 90, 94.

count his particular circumstances and needs, in the light of a discerning love."[3]

4. The time order of the community should include some brief daily common prayer and at times, in a way that is appropriate for each apostolic community, a longer period for prayer and prayerful discussion. Shared prayer, days of recollection, and the Spiritual Exercises in common are recognized as fruitful means for increasing union, since they provide the opportunity for reflecting before God on the mission of the community and, at the same time, express the apostolic character of our prayer.[4]

5. Our entire apostolic life should be examined with the spiritual discernment proper to the Exercises, so that we might increasingly put into practice what God expects of us and purify the motivation of our lives. One means available to us is the daily examination of conscience, which was recommended by St. Ignatius so that we might be continually guided by the practice of spiritual discernment.[5]

6. Since we need the grace of continual conversion of heart "to the love of the Father of mercies" that the purity and freedom of our lives in God's service might increase, all should frequent the Sacrament of Reconciliation. We should also willingly participate in communal penitential services and strive to promote the spirit of reconciliation in our communities.[6]

7. Dialogue with a spiritual director on a regular basis is a great help for growing in spiritual insight and learning

3 GC 32, D. 11, no. 36 [236]; see also G. 31, D. 14, nos. 11-12 [225-230]; D. 8, no. 35; *Cons,* [342, 582]; Father Arrupe, *ActRSJ,* XV, 486 (8).
4 GC 32, D. 11, no. 37 [237]; see also GC 31, D. 14, no. 15 [235].
5 GC 32, D. 11, no. 38 [238]; see also GC 31, D. 14, no. 13 [233].
6 GC 32, D. 11, no. 39 [239]; see also GC 31, D. 14, no. 8 [219].

discernment. Every Jesuit, especially during formation but also when he is engaged in an active apostolate, should make every effort to have a spiritual director with whom he can speak frequently and openly. The provincials should endeavour to identify and prepare spiritual fathers who are experienced in personal prayer and who have good judgment. This is especially true for the formation communities.[7]

8. The Spiritual Exercises are a privileged means for achieving renovation and union in the Society and for revitalizing our apostolic mission. They are a school of prayer and a time when a man has the spiritual experience of personally encountering Christ. The Spiritual Exercises should be made yearly by all, according to the method of Saint Ignatius, for eight successive days. Adaptations may be allowed because of particular circumstances; the provincial is to be the judge of the merits of each case. The circumstances of the annual retreat (such as silence, recollection, a location removed from ordinary work) should be managed in such a way that the Jesuit is able truly to renew his spiritual life through frequent and uninterrupted familiar conversation with God.[8]

9. The cult of the Sacred Heart of Jesus and devotion to Our Lady retain all their value. We should use these forms of spirituality, while taking account of the differences which exist in various parts of the world.[9]

CHASTITY

10. Among the natural and supernatural means which contribute more to the faithful fulfillment of one's oblation of chastity, Jesuits should give preference to those which are

---

7 GC 32, D. 11, no. 40 [240].
8 GC 32, D. 11, no. 42 [242] and GC 31, D. 14, no. 16 [236].
9 GC 32, D. 11, no. 43 [244]; see also GC 31, D. 14, no. 16 [236]; *CollDecr,* 55, §§ 1, 3; GC 31, D. 8, no. 35 [124].

positive, such as probity of life, generous dedication to one's assigned task, great desire for the glory of God, zeal for solid virtues and spiritual concerns, openness and simplicity in activity and in consulting with superiors, reaching out for richer cultural attainments, spiritual joy, and above all true charity. For all these things will of their nature more easily bring a man a really full and pure love for God and men which we earnestly desire.[10]

11. Nevertheless, mindful of the solitude of heart which constitutes part of the cross embraced through our vocation to follow Christ, and of our frailty which from youth to old age necessarily accompanies the development of chaste love, we cannot forget the ascetical norms which the Church and the Society in their wide experience maintain and which dangers against chastity require today no less than in the past.[11]

12. Sustained by the grace of God and mortified at all times, we should generously and strenuously devote ourselves to apostolic labor and know how to participate with moderation in the human contacts which our ministry involves, our visits and recreations, our reading and study of problems, our attendance at shows, and use of what is pleasurable, so that the testimony of our consecration to God will shine forth inviolate.[12]

13. Superiors should lovingly endeavor to lead back those whom they see or sense to be drawing away from the community. And all Jesuits should be prepared to cooperate with superiors in their solicitude, discreetly but in good time making known to them the difficulties and temptations of their confreres.[13]

---

10 GC 31, D. 16, no. 8, c [257].
11 GC 31, D. 16, no. 8, d [258].
12 GC 31, D. 16, no. 8, e [259].
13 GC 31, D. 16, no. 9, e [266].

POVERTY AND COMMON LIFE

14. Independence from the community in acquisition or expenditure, a vice with manifold disguises, cannot be tolerated. Every Jesuit must contribute to the community everything he receives by way of remuneration, stipend, alms, gift or in any other way. He receives from the community alone everything he needs. In the same way, by cheerfully and gratefully accepting the community's standard of living, each undertakes to support his brothers in their efforts to live and to love poverty. Those who are unwilling to observe this double law of common life, separate themselves from the fraternity of the Society in spirit if not in law. A peculium is not admitted among us.[14]

15. The standard of living of our houses should not be higher than that of a family of slender means whose providers must work hard for its support. The concrete exigencies of such a standard are to be discerned by individuals and communities in sincere deliberation with their superiors. It should look to food and drink, lodging and clothing, but also and perhaps especially to travel, recreation, use of automobiles, and of villas, vacations, etc. Some should scrutinize their leisure, sometimes such as hardly the rich enjoy.[15]

16. Our communities may not accumulate capital but must dispose of any anual surplus, according to a provincial plan which will look to the needs of communities, of apostolates, and of the poor.[16]

17. Even though our poverty is lived out in a community, it is the personal responsibility of each one, moved by a discerning love and without detriment to the common good, to

---

14 GC 32, D. 12, no. 8 [264] and Father Arrupe, *ActRSJ,* XV, 486 (no. 4).
15 GC 32, D. 12, no. 7 [263]; see also GC 31, D. 18, no. 13 [299].
16 GC 32, D. 12, no. 12 [268]; see also GC 32, D. 12, nos. 25, 27-29 [282, 284-286]; also GC 31, D. 18, no. 9 [295].

live and manifest poverty in practice, even by voluntarily living more frugally, under the guidance of superiors.[17]

OBEDIENCE

18. Dedicated to mission under obedience, we should leave the full and completely free disposal of ourselves to our superiors, desiring to be guided not by our own judgment and will, but by that indication of the divine will which is offered to us through obedience. Obedience is to be offered by all promptly, cheerfully and in a supernatural spirit, as to Christ.[18]

19. In our obedience, our responsibility and initiative too are sollicited. Therefore all should make their own the superior's command in a personal, responsible way, and with all diligence to "bring to the execution of commands and the discharge of assignments entrusted to them the resources of their minds and wills, and their gifts of nature and grace," while also "realizing that they are giving service to the upbuilding of Christ's Body according to God's design."[19]

20. The religious can, and sometimes should, set forth his own reasons and proposals to the superior. However, he does not necessarily have to understand fully why he is being sent. For vowed obedience, whether in humdrum or in heroic matters, is always an act of faith and freedom whereby the religious recognizes and embraces the will of God manifested to him by one who has authority to send him in the name of Christ.[20]

---

17 See GC 31, D. 18, no. 10 [266]; also GC 32, D. 12, no. 10 [266].
18 GC 31, D. 17, no. 9 [276-277]; *Cons,* [547; 618-619]; Letter on Obedience, no. 12.
19 GC 31, D. 17, no. 9 [277].
20 GC 31, D. 17, no. 11 [280] and GC 32, D. 11, no. 31 [231].

21. The account of conscience is of great importance for the spiritual governance of the Society, and its practice is to be esteemed and cultivated. Therefore, all should give an account of conscience to their superiors, according to the norms and spirit of the Society. In addition, the relationships between superiors and their brethren in the Society should be such as to encourage the account of conscience and conversation about spiritual matters.[21]

THE COMMUNITY

22. A Jesuit community must be above all a true faith community, in which the principal bond is love, that love by which our Lord and those to whom he has entrusted his mission of salvation are loved in a single act.[22]

23. All Jesuits, even those who must live apart because of the demands of their apostolate or for other justifiable reasons, should take an active part in the life of some community. To the extent that the bond with a community and its superior is more than merely juridical, that union of minds and hearts which is so desirable will be kept intact.[23]

24. Every community of the Society should have its own superior.[24]

25. Taking into account the mission it has been given, every community should after mature deliberation establish a time order for community life. This time order should be approved by the major superior and periodically revised.[25]

26. Customs which are more suitable for monastic life

21 GC 32, D. 11, no. 46 [247]; see also GC 31, D. 17, no. 8 [275].
22 GC 32, D. 11, no. 41 [241] and GC 31, D. 19, no. 5, a [317].
23 GC 32, D. 11, no. 44 [245].
24 GC 32, D. 11, no. 44 [246].
25 GC 32, D. 11, no. 47 [248]. See also GC 31, D. 19, nos. 5, f, 8, f [322, 343].

shall not be introduced into our community life, nor those
which are proper to seculars, and much less those which
manifest a worldly spirit. Let our relationships with all
other men be such as can rightly be expected from a man
consecrated to God and seeking the good of souls above all
things; and it should include a proper regard for genuine
fellowship with all other Jesuits.[26]

27. Since our communities are apostolic, they should be
oriented towards the service of others, particularly the poor,
and to cooperation with those who are seeking God or
working for greater justice in the world. For this reason,
under the leadership of superiors, communities should
periodically examine whether their way of living sufficiently
supports their apostolic mission and encourages hospitality.
They should also consider whether their style of life testifies
to simplicity, justice, and poverty.[27]

28. Communities will not be able to witness to Christian
love unless each member contributes to community life and
gives sufficient time and effort to the task. Only in this way
can an atmosphere be created which makes communication
possible and in which no one goes unnoticed or is
neglected.[28]

29. As far as apostolic work or other occupations for the
greater glory of God permit, each one, "esteeming all the
others as better than" himself, should be ready to help out
in the common work in the house.[29]

30. Every Ignatian apostolic community should fulfil the
conditions for a variety of forms of open and friendly communication on a spiritual level. Since it is a privileged way

---

26 GC 31, D. 19, no. 7, e [330-331].
27 GC 32, D. 11, no. 48 [249]. See also GC 31, D. 19, no. 7, e [332].
28 GC 32, D. 11, no. 49 [250].
29 GC 31, d. 19, no. 7, c [328].

to find God's will, the use of communal spiritual discernment is encouraged if the question at issue is of some importance and the necessary preconditions have been verified.[30]

31. Solidarity among communities in a province as well as fraternal charity require that communities be open to men of different ages, talent, and work.[31]

32. Keeping in mind apostolic poverty and our witness to those among whom we must live, our houses should be made suitable for apostolic work, study, prayer, relaxation of mind and a friendly spirit, so that Jesuits will feel at home in their own house. The dwelling and arrangement of the community should be such that it allows for needed privacy and encourages the spiritual, intellectual, and cultural development of community members. These are necessary conditions for the fulfilment of our apostolic mission.[32]

ONGOING FORMATION

33. Our continuing formation demands that definite periods of time be given to formal courses or simply to private study, whether in theology or other disciplines, as required for one's apostolate; also that, at determined times, all should be given sufficient opportunity for study and for reflection about their apostolic life.[33]

30 GC 32, D. 11, no. 50 [251].
31 GC 32, D. 11, no. 51 [252].
32 GC 31, D. 19, no. 7, f [333] and GC 32, D. 11, no. 52 [253].
33 GC 32, D. 6, nos. 20, 35 [152, 167].

PART II. ADAPTATION OF THE

FOUNDER'S CHARISM

TO MODERN TIMES
(continued)

B. Readings from Addresses of

His Holiness Pope Paul VI

to the 31st and 32nd

General Congregations

Editor's Introduction

St. Ignatius' desire to cooperate in the achievement of God's unfolding redemptive plan pertained not only to Christ as he was in Judaea 2,000 years ago, but also and prominently to the glorified Christ whom he saw at La Storta; that is, to the Christ still present and acting in the Church as his mystical body and in the pope as its head on earth. Ignatius had a deeply cherished concept of authority as descending, by delegation through a hierarchically ordered series in the Church, from Christ to the pope to the Jesuit general to the provincial to the rector of the local community and even to the minor officials whom he appoints (see *Constitutions,* [666] above). Ignatius desired to put an organized group at the service of the pope.

Because of this devotion to the Holy Father as the highest authority in the Church on earth, Ignatius expected all the professed members of his Society to have special devotion to the reigning pontiff, which all the professed members of the Society were to express, according to the Formula of the Institute, "by a special vow to carry out whatever the present and future pontiffs may order which pertains to the progress of souls and propagation of the faith . . . ; and to go . . . to whatsoever provinces"[1] a pope might send them. Ignatius made the details of this prescription more explicit in his *Constitutions;*[2] and he further expected all other members of his Society to share in this devotion.

Through the centuries many general congregations have reiterated this special devotion to the pope. Many sovereign pontiffs, too, have reciprocated it by their benevolent interest in the Society, its well-being, and its activities. This

---

1 Formula of the Institute, [**4**] [3], above on p. 7.

2 Esp. in *Cons,* [7, 527, 529, 612].

is especially true of our present Holy Father, Pope Paul VI. Before the 31st General Congregation began on May 7, 1965, he showed a keen interest in the proposals or "postulata" which were arriving in Rome from all the Society's worldwide provinces; and he addressed the members of the Congregation at its opening and again at its termination. He repeated this procedure at the beginning of the 32nd Congregation, and through Father General sent a message at its conclusion. It is therefore fitting that this vademecum should be brought to its close by excerpts from the Holy Father which convey salient features of his messages and missions to the Society of today.

READINGS FROM THE ADDRESS[1]

of May 7, 1965

Beloved Sons:

We are happy to receive you today, dear members of the Society of Jesus, and We greet you with Our warm and heartfelt good wishes.

You have gathered in Rome in accordance with the original law of your Society to form the General Congregation which will choose the successor of Father John Janssens, your Superior General, whose loss We mourn with you.

*

Everyone knows that Ignatius, your holy father and lawmaker, wanted your Society to be marked by a distinctive characteristic and to achieve results by a zeal rooted in virtue. Founded as the result of his unselfish and heaven-sent inspiration, the Society of Jesus was to be, in his plan, outstanding as the solid bulwark of the Church, the pledged protector of the Apostolic See, the militia trained in the practice of virtue.

Your glorious mark of distinction, the great claim to renown, with which you are endowed, is "to fight for God under the standard of the Cross, and to serve God alone and the Church, His spouse, under the Roman Pontiff, the Vicar of Christ on earth."[2]

*

---

1 For the complete text, see *DocsGC31and32,* pp. 311-316.
2 See Formula of the Institute, [3] [4].

157

The glorious pages of your history proclaim that the ambitions and lives of the sons have matched the ideals of their holy father, and that you have deserved the reputation and glory of being the legion ever faithful to the task of protecting the Catholic faith and the Apostolic See.

*

The tenor of your lives, as befits valiant soldiers of Christ, tireless workers beyond reproach, should be based solidly on the holiness of behavior which is characteristic of you, on an asceticism of the gospels, which is austere and noteworthy for its virility and strength. It should be permeated by an unwavering discipline which does not give way before individual inclinations, but instead is prompt and ready, reasonable and constant in all its ways and undertakings. In an army, if a line or unit does not keep to its assigned place, it is like an instrument or a voice out of tune.

*

Therefore, all should take care in their thinking, their teaching, their writing, their way of acting, not to conform to the spirit of the world, nor to let themselves be buffeted by every wind of doctrine[3] and not to give in to unreasonable novelties by following personal judgment beyond measure.

Instead, let each one of you consider it his chief honor to serve the Church, our Mother and Teacher; to follow not his own, but the counsel, the judgments, the projects of the hierarchy and to bring them to fruition; to be animated more by the spirit of cooperation than by that of privilege. The Church recognizes that you are most devoted sons, she especially cherishes you, honors you, and if We may use a bold expression, she reveres you. Now when more than ever, as a result of the decrees of the Second Vatican Council, the extent and the possibilities of the apostolate are seen to

---

3 See Eph. 4:14.

be so vast, the holy Church of God needs your holiness of life, your wisdom, your understanding of affairs, your dedication to labor, and she asks of you that, holding on most tenaciously to the faith of old, you bring forth from the treasure of your heart new things and old for the increase of God's world-wide glory and for the salvation of the human race, in the name of Our Lord Jesus Christ whom God has glorified and to whom He has given a name which is above every name.[4]

*

We gladly take this opportunity to lay serious stress, however briefly, on a matter of grave importance: We mean the fearful danger of atheism threatening human society. Needless to say it does not always show itself in the same manner but advances and spreads under many forms. Of these, the anti-God movement is clearly to be reckoned the most pernicious: not content with a thoroughgoing denial of God's existence, this violent movement against God attacks theism, aiming at the extirpation of the sense of religion and all that is good and holy. There is also philosophical atheism that denies God's existence or maintains that God is unknowable, hedonistic atheism, atheism that rejects all religious worship or honor, reckoning it superstitious, profitless and irksome to reverence and serve the Creator of us all or to obey His law. Their adherents live without Christ, having no hope of the promise, and without God in this world.[6] This is the atheism spreading today, openly or covertly, frequently masquerading as cultural, scientific or social progress.

It is the special characteristic of the Society of Jesus to be champion of the Church and holy religion in adversity. To it We give the charge of making a stout, united stand

---

4 See Phil. 2:9.

6 See Eph. 2:12.

against atheism, under the leadership, and with the help of St. Michael, prince of the heavenly host. His very name is the thunder-peal or token of victory.

We bid the companions of Ignatius to muster all their courage and fight this good fight, making all the necessary plans for a well-organized and successful campaign. It will be their task to do research, to gather information of all kinds, to publish material, to hold discussions among themselves, to prepare specialists in the field, to pray, to be shining examples of justice and holiness, skilled and well-versed in an eloquence of word and example made bright by heavenly grace, illustrating the words of St. Paul: "My message and my preachings had none of the persuasive force of 'wise' argumentation, but the convincing power of the Spirit."[7]

You will carry it out with greater readiness and enthusiasm if you keep in mind that this work in which you are now engaged and to which you will apply yourselves in the future with renewed vigor is not something arbitrarily taken up by you, but a task solemnly entrusted to you by the Church and by the Supreme Pontiff.

*

With these heartfelt greetings to you all, members of the Society of Jesus, the festive and happy group that surrounds us today, We impart our apostolic blessing on all of you, on all your undertakings, and on the great hope which sets your hearts on fire for pure and lofty aims to be achieved.

---

7 1 Cor. 2:4.

READINGS FROM THE ADDRESS[1]

of November 16, 1966

Beloved sons:

It was Our desire that you concelebrate and share with us in the Eucharistic Sacrifice before departing, each to his own land, at the conclusion of your General Congregation and before setting out from Rome, the center of Catholic unity, for the four corners of the world. We wanted to greet each and every one of you cordially, to hearten and encourage you, and to bless each of you, your entire Society and your various works which you undertake for the glory of God and in the service of Holy Church. We desire to renew in your hearts in an almost palpable and solemn way the sense of the apostolic mandate that characterizes and strengthens your mission.

*

For that reason, We have chosen this place that is sacred and awe-inspiring in its beauty, its majesty and especially in the significance of its paintings. This is a place especially venerable by reason of our prayer pronounced here, a most humble prayer but a Pope's prayer, . . .

*

By this prayer in which we shall implore the Holy Spirit together, all those things which you have so carefully done during this most important period will receive a special approval. You have subjected your Society and all its works to a critical examination, as though concluding four centuries of its history just after the close of the Second Vatican Council, and beginning a new age of your religious life with a fresh outlook and with new proposals.

---

1 For the complete text, see *DocsGC31and32,* pp. 317-324.

This meeting therefore, my brothers and most beloved sons, takes on a particular historical significance in that it is given to you and to us to define by means of reciprocal clarification the relationship which exists and which should exist between Holy Church and the Society of Jesus. Through divine mandate We exercise the pastoral guidance of this Church and sum up in ourselves and represent it. What is this relationship? It is up to you and to us to furnish a reply, which will follow a twofold division:

1) Do you, sons of St. Ignatius, soldiers of the Society of Jesus, want even today and tomorrow and always to be what you were from your beginnings right up to today, for the service of the Catholic Church and of this Apostolic See? There would be no reason for asking this question had not certain reports and rumors come to our attention about your Society just as about other religious families as well, which—and We cannot remain silent on this—have caused us amazement and in some cases, sorrow.

What strange and evil suggestions have caused a doubt to arise in certain parts of your widespread Society whether it should continue to be the Society conceived and founded by that holy man, and built on very wise and very firm norms? The tradition of several centuries ripened by most careful experience and confirmed by authoritative approvals has shaped the Society for the glory of God, the defence of the Church and the admiration of men. In the minds of some of your members, has the opinion really prevailed to the effect that all human things, which are generated in time and inexorably used up in time, are subject to an absolute law of history as though in Catholicism there were no charism of permanent truth and of invincible stability? This rock of the Apostolic See is the symbol and foundation of this charism.

*

Perhaps some have been deceived into thinking that in order to spread the Gospel of Christ they must take on the ways of the world, its manner of thinking and acting, and its worldly view of life. On the basis of naturalistic norms they judged the customs of this age and thus forgot that the rightful and apostolic approach of the hearald of Christ to men, who brings God's message to men, cannot be such an assimilation as to make the salt lose its tang and the apostle his own virtue.

These were clouds on the horizon, but they have been dispersed in large measure by the conclusions of your Congregation! It was with great joy that we learned that you, in the strong rectitude which has always inspired your will, after a careful and sincere study of your history, of your vocation, and of your experience, have decreed to hold fast to your fundamental constitutions and not to abandon your tradition which in your keeping has had a continual effectiveness and vitality.

*

2) And now the second question arises, that of determining the relationship of your Society to the Church and in a special way to the Holy See. There is a second question which We can almost read on your lips: does the Church, does the successor of St. Peter, think that the Society of Jesus is still their special and most faithful militia? . . .

Here, my dear sons, is our reply: Yes! We have faith and we retain our faith in you; and thus We give you a mandate for your apostolic works; We show you our affection and gratitude; and We give you our blessing.

In this solemn and historic hour you have confirmed with your new proposals that you wish to cling very closely to your Institute, which, when the restorative work of the Council of Trent burned bright, put itself at the service of the Catholic Church. Thus it is easy and enjoyable for us to repeat the words and acts of our predecessors at this time which is different but no less a time of renewal of the life of the Church, following the Second Vatican Council. It is a joy for us to assure you that as long as your Society will be intent on striving for excellence in sound doctrine and in

163

holiness of religious life and will offer itself as a most effective instrument for the defense and spread of the Catholic Faith, this Apostolic See, and with it, certainly the whole Church, will hold it most dear.

*

The Church accepts the promise of your work and the offer of your life; and since you are soldiers of Christ, it calls you and commits you to difficult and sacred struggles in His name, today, more than ever.

Do you not see how much support the faith needs today, what open adherence, what clear exposition, what tireless preaching, what erudite explanation, how much testimony full of love and generosity?

Do you not see what opportunities are furnished by modern ecumenism to the servant and apostle of the holy Catholic Church for happily creating close relationships with others, for entering prudently into discussions, for patiently proposing explanations, for enlarging the field of charity?

Who is better suited than you to devote study and effort in order that our separated brethren may know and understand us, may listen to us and with us share the glory, the joy, and the service of the mystery of unity in Christ our Lord?

As for the infusion of Christian principles in the modern world as described in the now celebrated pastoral constitution *Gaudium et Spes,* will it not find among you able, prudent and strong specialists? And will not the devotion which you show to the Sacred Heart be still a most effective instrument in contributing to the spiritual and moral renewal of this world that the Second Vatican Council has urged, and to accomplishing fruitfully the mission entrusted to you to confront atheism?

Will you not dedicate yourselves with new zeal to the education of youth in secondary schools and universities, whether ecclesiastical or civil, something which has always been for you a cause of high praise and eminent merit? You should keep in mind that you have been entrusted with many young persons who one day will be able to render precious service to the Church and to human society, if they have received a sound formation.

And what shall we say of the missions? These missions where so many of your members labor admirably, bend every effort, put up with hardships and strive to make the name of Jesus shine forth like the sun of salvation, are they not entrusted to you by this apostolic see as they were once to Francis Xavier, in the assurance of having in you heralds of the faith sure and daring, full of the charity that your interior life renders inexhaustible, comforting and beyond expression.

And finally, what about the world? This ambivalent world which has two faces: the one is that of the compact entered into by all who turn from light and grace; the other, that of the vast human family for which the Father sent His Son and for which the Son sacrificed Himself. This world of today is so powerful and so weak, so hostile and so well disposed; does not this world call you and us to itself, imploring and urging us to a task to be fulfilled? Does not this world, groaning and trembling in this place, in the sight of Christ, now cry out to all of you: "Come, come; the longing and the hunger of Christ await you; come, for it is time."

Yes it is time, my dear sons; Go forth in faith and ardor; Christ chooses you, the Church sends you, the Pope blesses you.

READINGS FROM THE ADDRESS[1]

of December 3, 1974

Esteemed and beloved Fathers of the Society of Jesus,

As we receive you today, there is renewed for us the joy and trepidation of May 7, 1965, when the Thirty-first General Congregation of your Society began, and that of November 15 of the following year, at its conclusion. We have great joy because of the outpouring of sincere paternal love which every meeting between the Pope and the sons of St. Ignatius cannot but stir up. This is especially true because we see the witness of Christian apostolate and of fidelity which you give us and in which we rejoice. But there is also trepidation for the reasons of which we shall presently speak to you. The inauguration of the 32nd General Congregation is a special event, and it is usual for us to have such a meeting on an occasion like this; but this meeting has a far wider and more historic significance. It is the whole Ignatian Society that has gathered at Rome before the Pope after a journey of more than four hundred years, and is reflecting, perhaps, on the prophetic words that were heard in the vision of La Storta: "I will be favorable to you in Rome."

*

We realize the special seriousness of the present moment. It demands of you more than a routine performance of your function: it demands an examination of the present state of your Society, one that will be a careful synthesis, free and complete, to see how it stands with regard to the difficulties and problems that beset it today. It is an act that

---

1 For the complete text, see *DocsGC31and32,* pp. 519-536.

must be accomplished with extreme lucidity and with a supernatural spirit—to compare your identity with what is happening in the world and in the Society itself—listening exclusively, under the guidance and illumination of the magisterium, to the voice of the Holy Spirit, and consequently with a disposition of humility, of courage, and of resoluteness to decide on the course of action to be adopted, lest there be prolonged a state of uncertainty that would become dangerous. All this with great confidence.

And we give you the confirmation of our confidence: we love you sincerely, and we judge that you are able to effect that renewal and new balance which we all desire.

This is the meaning of today's meeting, and we want you to reflect on it. We already made known our thought in this regard through the letters that the Cardinal Secretary of State sent in our name on March 26, 1970, and on February 15, 1973, and with that letter of September 13, 1973, *In Paschae Sollemnitate,* which we sent to the General and through him to all the members of the Society.

Continuing along the line of thought of the last-mentioned document, which we hope has been meditated and reflected upon by you, as was our wish, we speak to you today with special affection and a particular urgency.

*

And it seems to us, as we listen in this hour of anxious expectation and of intense attention "to what the Spirit is saying" to you and to us (see Rev. 2:7 ff.), that there arise in our heart three questions which we feel bound to answer: "Where do you come from?", "Who are you?", "Where are you going?"

So we stand here before you, like a milestone, to measure in one sweeping glance, the journey you have already made.

I.   Hence, *where do you come from?* Our thought goes back to that complex sixteenth century, when the foundations of modern civilization and culture were being laid, and the Church, threatened by schism, began a new era of religious and social renewal founded on prayer and on the love of God and the brethren, that is, on the search for genuine holiness. It was a moment bound up with a new concept of man of the world, which often—although this was not the most genuine humanism—attempted to relegate God to a place outside the course of life and history. It was a world which took on new dimensions from recent geographical discoveries, and hence in very many of its aspects—upheavals, rethinking, analyses, reconstructions, impulses, aspirations, etc.—was not unlike our own.

Placed against this stormy and splendid background is the figure of St. Ignatius. Yes, where do you come from? And we seem to hear a united cry—a "voice like the sound of the ocean" (Rev 1:15)—resounding from the depths of the centuries from all your confreres: We come from Ignatius Loyola, our Founder—we come from him who has made an indelible imprint not only on the Order but also on the spirituality and the apostolate of the Church.

With him, we come from Manresa, from the mystical cave which witnessed the successive ascents of his great spirit: from the serene peace of the beginner to the purifications of the dark night of the soul, and finally to the great mystical graces of the visions of the Trinity (see Hugo Rahner, *The Spirituality of St. Ignatius Loyola: An Account of Its Historical Development* [Westminster, Md., 1953]), ch. 3.

There began at that time the first outlines of the Spiritual Exercises, that work which over the centuries has formed souls, orienting them to God, and which, among other things, teaches the lesson of treating "the Creator and Lord with great openheartedness and generosity, offering him all one's will and liberty, so that his divine Majesty may avail himself, in accordance with his most holy will, of the person and of all that he has."

*

II.   We know then *who you are.* As we summarized in our Letter, *In Paschae Sollemnitate,* you are members of an Order that is religious, apostolic, priestly, and united with the Roman Pontiff by a special bond of love and service, in the manner described in the *Formula Instituti.*

You are religious, and therefore men of prayer, of the evangelical imitation of Christ, and endowed with a supernatural spirit, guaranteed and protected by the religious vows of poverty, chastity and obedience. These vows are not an obstacle to the freedom of the person, as though they were a relic of periods that have sociologically been superseded, but rather a witness to the clear desire for freedom in the spirit of the Sermon on the Mount. By means of these commitments, the one who is called as Vatican II has emphasized—"in order to derive more abundant fruit from the grace of Baptism . . . intends to be freed from the obstacles which might draw him away from the fervor of charity and the perfection of divine worship and consecrates himself to the service of God" (*Lumen Gentium,* 44; see also *Perfectae Caritatis,* 12-14).

*

You are, moreover, *apostles,* that is, preachers of the Gospel, sent in every direction in accordance with the most authentic and genuine character of the Society. You are men whom Christ himself sends into the whole world to spread his holy doctrine among the people of every state and condition (see *Spiritual Exercises,* [145].

*

You are likewise *priests*: this, too, is an essential character of the Society, without forgetting the ancient and established tradition of enlisting the help of Brothers who are not in Sacred Orders and who have always had an honored and effective role in the Society. Priesthood was formally required by the Founder for all professed religious, and this with good reason, because the priesthood is necessary for the Order he instituted with the special purpose of the sanctification of men through the word and the sacraments. Effectively, the sacerdotal character is required by your dedication to the active life—we repeat—*pleno sensu*. It is from the charism of the Order of priesthood, which conforms a man to Christ sent by the Father, that there principally springs the apostolic character of the mission to which, as Jesuits, you are deputed. . . .

You are priests who serve or minister the grace of God through the sacraments; priests who receive the power and have the duty to share organically in the apostolic work of sustaining and uniting the Christian community, especially with the celebration of the Eucharist.

*

And finally you are *united with the Pope* by a special vow: since this union with the Successor of Peter, which is the principal bond of the members of the Society, has always given the assurance—indeed it is the visible sign—of your communion with Christ, the first and supreme head of the Society which by its very name is his—the Society of Jesus. And it is union with the Pope that has always rendered the members of the Society truly free, that is, placed under the direction of the Spirit, fit for all missions —even the most arduous and most distant ones—not hemmed in by the narrow conditions of time and place, and endowed with truly Catholic and universal energy.

In the combination of this fourfold note we see displayed all the wonderful richness and adaptability which has characterized the Society during the centuries as the Society of those "sent" by the Church. Hence there have come theological research and teaching, hence the apostolate of preaching, of spiritual assistance, of publications and writings, of the direction of groups, and of formation by means of the word of God and the Sacrament of Reconciliation in accordance with the special and characteristic duty committed to you by your holy Founder. Hence there have come the social apostolate and intellectual and cultural activity which extends from schools for the solid and complete education of youth all the way to all the levels of advanced university studies and scholarly research. Hence the *puerorum ac rudium in christianismo institutio,* which St. Ignatius gives to his sons, from the very first moment of his *Quinque Capitula,* or *First Sketch,* as one of their specific aims. Hence the missions, a concrete and moving testimony of the "mission" of the Society. Hence the solicitude for the poor, for the sick, for those on the margins of society. Wherever in the Church, even in the most difficult and extreme fields, in the crossroads of ideologies, in the front line of social conflict, there has been and there is confrontation between the deepest desires of man and the perennial message of the Gospel, there also there have been, and there are, Jesuits.

*

And why then do you doubt? You have a spirituality strongly traced out, an unequivocal identity and a centuries-old confirmation which was based on the validity of methods, which, having passed through the crucible of history, still bear the imprint of the strong spirit of St. Ignatius. Hence there is absolutely no need to place in doubt the fact that a more profound commitment to the way up till now followed—to the special charism—will be the source of spiritual and apostolic fruitfulness. It is true that there is today widespread in the Church the temptation characteristic of our time: systematic doubt, uncertainty about one's identity, desire for change, independence, and individualism. The difficulties that you have noticed are those that today seize Christians in general in the face of the profound cultural change which strikes at one's very sense of God. Yours are the difficulties of all today's apostles, those who experience the longing to proclaim the Gospel and the difficulty of translating it into a language accessible to modern man; they are the difficulties of other religious orders. We understand the doubts and the true

171

and serious difficulties that some of you are undergoing. You are at the head of that interior renewal which the Church is facing in this secularized world, especially after the Second Vatican Council. Your Society is, we say, the test of the vitality of the Church throughout the centuries; it is perhaps one of the most meaningful crucibles in which are encountered the difficulties, the temptations, the efforts, the perpetuity and the successes of the whole Church.

Certainly it is a crisis of suffering, and perhaps of growth, as has been said many times. But we, in our capacity as Vicar of Christ, who must confirm the brethren in faith (see Lk 22:32), and likewise you, who have the heavy responsibility of consciously representing the aspirations of your confreres—all of us must be vigilant so that the necessary adaptation will not be accomplished to the detriment of the fundamental identity or essential character of the role of the Jesuit as is described in the *Formula Instituti,* as the history and particular spirituality of the Order propose it, and as the authentic interpretation of the very needs of the times seem still today to require it. This image must not be altered; it must not be distorted.

*

You are as well aware as we are that today there appears within certain sectors of your ranks a strong state of uncertainty, indeed a certain fundamental questioning of your very identity. The figure of the Jesuit, as we have traced it out in its principal aspects, is essentially that of a spiritual leader, an educator of his contemporaries in Catholic life, within, as we have said, his proper role, as a priest and as an apostle. But we are asking, and you are asking yourselves, as a conscientious verification and as a reassuring confirmation, what is the present state of the life of prayer, of contemplation, of simplicity of life, of poverty, of the use of supernatural means? What is the state of acceptance and loyal witness in regard to the fundamental points of

Catholic faith and moral teaching as set forth by the ecclesiastical magisterium? The will to collaborate with full trust in the work of the Pope? Have not the "clouds on the horizon" which we saw in 1966, although "in a great measure dispersed" by the Thirty-first General Congregation (*AAS* 58 (1966), p. 1174), unfortunately continued to cast a certain shadow on the Society? Certain regrettable actions, which would make one doubt whether the man were still a member of the Society, have happened much too frequently and are pointed out to us from many sides, especially from bishops of dioceses; and they exercise a sad influence on the clergy, on other religious, and on the Catholic laity. These facts require from us and from you an expression of sorrow, certainly not for the sake of dwelling on them, but for seeking together the remedies, so that the Society will remain, or return to being, what is needed, what it must be in order to respond to the intention of the Founder and to the expectations of the Church today.

*

III. Therefore, *where are you going?* The question cannot remain unanswered. You have in fact been asking it for some time, asking it with lucidity, perhaps with risk.

The goal to which you are tending, and of which this General Congregation is the opportune sign of the times, is and must be without doubt the pursuit of a healthy, balanced, and suitable *aggiornamento* to the right desires of our day in essential fidelity to the specific character of the Society and in respect for the charism of your Founder. This was the desire of the Second Vatican Council, with the Decree *Perfectae Caritatis* which hoped for "the continued return to the sources of every Christian life and to the original spirit of institutes, and the adaptation of the institutes themselves to the changed conditions of the times" (*op. cit.,* 2). We would like to inspire you with full confidence and encourage you to keep pace with the attitudes of the world of today, recalling to you, nevertheless, as we did in a general way in the Apostolic Exhortation *Evangelica Testificatio*, that such necessary renewal would not be effective if it departed from the particular identity of your religious family which is so clearly described in your fundamental rule or *Formula Instituti*.

*

Hence we encourage you with all our heart to pursue the *aggiornamento* willed so clearly and authoritatively by the Church. But at the same time, we are all aware of both its importance and its innate risk. The world in which we live places in crisis our religious outlook and sometimes even our option of faith: we live in a dazzling perspective of worldly humanism, bound up with a rationalistic and irreligious attitude with which man wants to complete his personal and social perfection exclusively by his own efforts. On the other hand for us, who are men of God, it is a question of the divinization of man in Christ, through the choice of the Cross and of the struggle against evil and sin.

*

Hence, in the road that opens before you in this remaining part of the century, marked by the Holy Year as a hopeful presage for a radical conversion to God, we propose to you the double charism of the apostle—the charism which must guarantee your identity and constantly illumine your teaching, your centers of study, your periodical publications. On the one hand, *fidelity*—not sterile and static, but living and fruitful—to the faith and to the institution of your Founder, in order that you may remain the salt of the earth and the light of the world (see Mt 5:13, 14). Guard what has been entrusted to you (see 1 Tim 6:20; 2 Tim 1:14).

On the other hand, there is the charism of love, that is of generous *service* to all men, our brethren traveling with us towards the future. It is that anxiety of Paul which every true apostle feels burning within him: "I made myself all things to all men in order to save some at any cost . . . I try to be helpful to everyone at all times, not anxious for my own advantage but for the advantage of everybody else, so that they may be saved" (1 Cor 9:22; 10:33).

Perfection lies in the simultaneous presence of two charisms—fidelity and service—without letting one have the advantage over the other. This is something that is certainly difficult, but it is possible. Today the attraction of the second charism is very strong: the precedence of action over being, of activity over contemplation, of concrete existence over theoretical speculation, which has led from a deductive theology to an inductive one; and all this could cause one to think that the two aspects of fidelity and love are mutually opposed. But such is not the case, as you know. Both proceed from the Holy Spirit, who is love. People are never loved too much, provided they are loved only in the love and with the love of Christ.

*

We wish to indicate to you some further orientations which you can develop in your reflections:

A) *Discernment,* for which Ignatian spirituality especially trains you, must always sustain you in the difficult quest for the synthesis of the two charisms, the two poles of your life. You will have to be able always to distinguish with absolutely lucid clarity between the demands of the world and those of the Gospel, of its paradox of death and life, of Cross and Resurrection, of folly and wisdom. Take your direction from the judgment of St. Paul: "But because of Christ, I have come to consider all these advantages that I had as disadvantages. Not only that, but I believe nothing can happen that will outweigh the supreme advantage of knowing Christ and the power of his resurrection and to share his sufferings by reproducing the pattern of his death. That is the way I can hope to take my place in the resurrection of the dead" (Phil. 3:7-8, 10-11). We recall always that a supreme criterion is the one given by Our Lord:

"You will be able to tell them by their fruits" (Mt. 7:16); and the effort which must guide your discernment will be that of being docile to the voice of the Spirit in order to produce the fruit of the Spirit, which is "love, joy, peace, patience, kindness, goodness, trustfulness, gentleness and self-control" (Gal 5:22).

B) It will also be opportune to remember the need to make a proper *basic choice* among the many appeals that come to you from the apostolate in the modern world. Today—it is a fact—one notes the difficulty of making properly thought-out and decisive choices; perhaps there is a fear that full self-realization will not be achieved. Hence there is the desire to be everything, the desire to do everything and to follow indiscriminately all the human and Christian vocations—those of the priest and the lay person, those of the Religious Institutes and of the Secular Institutes—applying oneself to spheres that are not one's own. Hence then arise lack of satisfaction, improvisation and discouragement. But you have a precise vocation, that which we have just recalled, and an unmistakably specific character in your spirituality and in your apostolic vocation. And this is what you must profoundly study in its main guidelines.

C) Finally, we once more remind you of *availability of obedience*. This, we would say, is the characteristic feature of the Society: "In other Orders," St. Ignatius wrote in his famous letter of March 26, 1553, "one can find advantages in fastings, vigils, and other austerities . . .; but I greatly desire, beloved brothers, that those who serve our Lord God in this Society may be marked by the purity and perfection of obedience, with true renunciation of our wills and the abnegation of our judgments."

*

Beloved sons!

At the end of this encounter we believe that we have given you some indications concerning the path which you must take in today's world; and we have also wanted to indicate to you the path which you must take in the world of the future. Know it, approach it, serve it, love it—this world; and in Christ it will be yours. Look at it with the same eyes as St. Ignatius did; note the same spiritual requirements; use the same weapons: prayer, a choice for the side of God, of his glory, the practice of asceticism, absolute availability. We think that we are not asking you too much when we express the desire that the Congregation should profoundly study and restate the essential elements (*essentialia*) of the Jesuit vocation in such a way that all your confreres will be able to recognize themselves, to strengthen their commitment, to rediscover their identity, to experience again their particular vocation, and to recast their proper community union. The moment requires it, the Society expects a decisive voice. Do not let that voice be lacking!

We are following with the most lively interest this work of yours, work which ought to have a great influence upon your holiness, your apostolate, and your fidelity to your charism and to the Church. We accompany your work especially with our prayer that the light of the Holy Spirit, the Spirit of the Father and of the Son, may illumine you, strengthen you, guide you, rouse you, and give you the incentive to follow ever more closely Christ crucified.

*

This is the way, this is the way, brothers and sons. Forward, *in Nomine Domini*. Let us walk together, free, obedient, united to each other in the love of Christ, for the greater glory of God. Amen.

READINGS FROM THE ADDRESS[1]

of March 7, 1975

Beloved Members of the Society of Jesus:

Almost three months ago, on the third of last December, it was a consolation for Us to receive in audience all the Fathers the Society of Jesus who are members of the 32nd General Congregation just when they were undertaking their work. . . . We now have a great occasion for rejoicing since we have yet another opportunity of once again giving evidence of our great, paternal and sincere good will for this religious order that is so clearly joined with Us and is certainly very dear to Us.

For our part, We admit that We were impelled by the very spirit of love, by which We embrace all of you, to interpose our authority with the superiors of your Society— as you well know—in rather recent circumstances. We thought that this action had to be taken because of our consciousness that We are the supreme protector and guardian of the Formula of the Institute, as well as the Shepherd of the Universal Church. Actually, at that time We were not a little pleased by the fact that the members of the General Congregation favorably understood the force and meaning of our recommendations and showed that they received them with a willingness to carry them out. Now We wish once again to cite the words of the Apostle Paul: "I wrote (what) I did . . . (confident that) you all know that I could never be happy, unless you were. When I wrote to you, in deep distress and anguish of mind, and in tears, it was not to make you feel hurt but to let you know how much love I have for you" (2 Cor. 2:3-4).

---

1 For the complete text, see *DocsGC31and32,* pp. 542-544.

Some of you, perhaps in order to inject new vigor into the life of your Society, thought that it would be necessary to introduce substantially new elements into the Formula of the Institute, that is, into its primary norms or into its adaptation to the present social milieu. For our part, We cannot allow changes based on such reasoning to enter into your religious institute, which is of its very nature so special and so fully approved, not only by historical experience but also by hardly doubtful indications of divine protection. We feel that the Society must indeed be adapted and adjusted to this age of ours and must be enriched with new vitality, but always in accord with the principles of the Gospel and the Institute. It must not be transformed or deformed.

*

At the close of this Congregation, We gladly take advantage of the occasion to give this reminder to each and every son of St. Ignatius, scattered as they are throughout the world: Be loyal! This loyalty, which is freely and effectively shown to the Formula of the Institute, will safeguard the original and true form of the companions of Ignatius and strengthen the fruitfulness of their apostolate.

*

When We consider the great quantity of works which have been entrusted to you and which demand minds of proven maturity of judgment and firm wills outstanding in humility and generosity, it is our wish that all the members of the Society of Jesus be supported by supernatural helps and that they always rely on them!

*

Therefore We exhort all the companions of Ignatius to continue with renewed zeal to carry out all the works and endeavors upon which they have so eagerly embarked in the service of the Church and that they be aware of the importance of their tasks while at the same time they rely on the help and assistance of God who alone suffices just as he alone was always sufficient for Ignatius and Francis Xavier in the midst of the great needs which they experienced. You should be aware of the fact that not only the eyes of contemporary men in general but also and especially those of so many members of other religious orders and congregations and even those of the universal Church are turned toward you. May such grandly conceived hopes, then, not be frustrated! Go, therefore, and proceed in the name of the Lord. As sons and brethren, go forth always and only in the name of the Lord.

With our Apostolic Blessing, We wish to confirm this desire of our heart.

Bathroom Design

teNeues

Imprint

Produced by fusion publishing GmbH, Berlin   www.fusion-publishing.com

Edited by Verena von Holtum, teNeues Verlag; Editorial Coordination by Sandra-Mareike Kreß, fusion publishing
Text by Nicolas Uphaus; Translations by Bochert Translations
Layout by Manuela Roth, fusion publishing; Imaging & Pre-press by Jan Hausberg, fusion publishing

Photos (page): Courtesy AF NEW YORK (AF NEW YORK, p. 149), Courtesy Agape srl (Agape, pp. 64-65, 77, 88, 100-103, 110 top, 112-113, 125, 138, 174-175, 180), Courtesy Antrax IT srl (Antrax IT, p. 178), Courtesy ArtQuitect (ArtQuitect, pp. 124, 176-177), Courtesy Boffi S.p.A. (Boffi, pp. 4, 9, 22-25, 60-63, 72-73), Courtesy Cesana SpA (Cesana, pp. 14, 89, 114-115), Courtesy Duravit AG (Duravit, pp. 7, 11, 16-17, 46-49, 91, 96, 104, 126, 136, 139, 166), Courtesy ESPRIT home bath concept über Kludi GmbH & Co. KG (ESPRIT home/Kludi, pp. 32-35, 78-79, 140), Courtesy Falper Srl (Falper, pp. 26-31, 98-99, 107, 109, 134-135), Courtesy Franz Kaldewei GmbH & Co. KG (Kaldewei, pp. 3, 8, 67-69, 85, 92, 118-119), Courtesy GUNNI & TRENTINO (TRENTINO, pp. 128-129, 141), Courtesy Hansgrohe AG/Axor (Hansgrohe, pp. 15, 18-21, 75, 80-81, 90, 116, 122, 148, 150-153, 156-157), Courtesy HOESCH Design GmbH (HOESCH, pp. 70-71, 97, 105, 108, 123), Courtesy Inter IKEA Systems B.V. 2009 (IKEA, pp. 36-39), Courtesy INTACT-BAD GmbH/photographed by Uwe Spöring (INTACT-BAD, pp. 84, 137, 184-221), Courtesy JOOP! LIVING (JOOP! LIVING, pp. 5, 40-45, 67, 82-83, 117, 142-143, 162-163, 181), Courtesy Keramag AG (Keramag, pp. 74, pp. 130 top, 144, 182-183), Courtesy Koralle Sanitärprodukte GmbH (Koralle, pp. 120 top, 121), Courtesy Olympia Ceramica srl (Olympia, pp. 12, 13, 66, 130 bottom, 131), Courtesy ORAS GmbH & Co. KG (ORAS, pp. 10, 106, 132-133, 154-155, 164-165, 172-173), Didier Grieu/Courtesy THG Paris (THG Paris, pp. 50-52, 86-87, 158-160 top, 169), Courtesy Villeroy & Boch AG (Villeroy & Boch, pp. 6, 54-59, 94-95, 110 bottom, 111, 120 bottom, 127, 145-147, 160 bottom, 161, 167-168, 170-171, 179)

Cover photo: Didier Grieu/Courtesy THG Paris (THG Paris)

Back cover photos from top to bottom: Courtesy ORAS GmbH & Co. KG (ORAS, picture 1&2); Courtesy INTACT-BAD GmbH/photographed by Uwe Spöring (INTACT-BAD); Courtesy Franz Kaldewei GmbH & Co. KG (Kaldewei); Courtesy Cesana SpA (Cesana)

Published by teNeues Publishing Group

teNeues Verlag GmbH + Co. KG
Am Selder 37
47906 Kempen, Germany
Tel.: 0049-(0)2152-916-0
Fax: 0049-(0)2152-916-111
E-mail: books@teneues.de

teNeues Publishing Company
16 West 22nd Street
New York, NY 10010, USA
Tel.: 001-212-627-9090
Fax: 001-212-627-9511

teNeues Publishing UK Ltd.
21 Marlowe Court, Lymer Avenue
London, SE19 1LP
Great Britain
Tel.: 0044-208-670-7522
Fax: 0044-208-670-7523

teNeues France S.A.R.L.
39, rue de Billets
18250 Henrichemont
France
Tel.: 0033-2-48269348
Fax: 0033-1-70723482

Press department: arehn@teneues.de
Tel.: 0049-2152-916-202

www.teneues.com

ISBN: 978-3-8327-9399-9

Bibliographic information published by the Deutsche Nationalbibliothek.
The Deutsche Nationalbibliothek lists this publication in the Deutsche Nationalbibliografie; detailed bibliographic data are available in the Internet at http://dnb.d-nb.de.

STYLE

MATERIAL

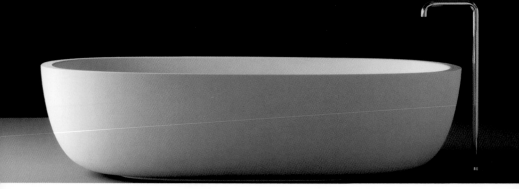

ELEMENTS

CUSTOM MADE

Introduction

From a functional room and a place to wash, the bathroom has evolved into a private relaxation oasis where body and mind alike are calmed and rejuvenated. This is reflected in a minimal and well thought-out design that focuses on the element water.

Archaic simple forms and technical perfection complement one another brilliantly. Likewise, the modern bathroom is not considered as a separate room anymore, but rather integrated with the bedroom—a combination which is evident inherently as well as practically. This fusion is shown in new materials and a warmer, more comfortable design that harmonizes with the new meaning of the bathroom perfectly.

The materials must be durable, easy to maintain and at the same time satisfy at a sensory level, therefore pleasing to the eye and nice to the touch. With the combination of contrasting elements a tension is built up that turns the bathroom into a holistic experience. From the wall design to the tap, the complete individual dream bathroom today can be a combination of a variety of components. The result is a room in which necessity and luxury are most closely connected.

Nicolas Uphaus

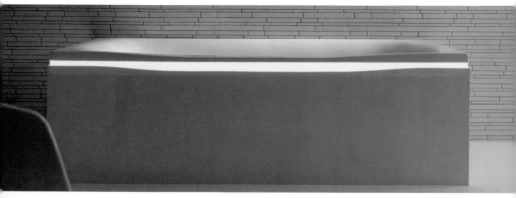

Einleitung

Vom zweckmäßigen Raum zur Körperreinigung hat sich das Bad zu einer privaten Entspannungsoase entwickelt, in der Körper und Geist gleichermaßen zur Ruhe kommen und regenerieren können. Dies spiegelt sich in einer reduzierten und durchdachten Gestaltung wider, die das Element Wasser in den Fokus rückt.

Archaische Grundformen und technische Perfektion ergänzen sich prächtig. Ebenfalls wird das moderne Bad nicht mehr als separater Raum betrachtet, sondern schließt sich mit dem Schlafbereich zusammen – eine Kombination, die emotional wie auch praktisch sinnfällig ist. Von diesem Zusammenschluss zeugen neue Materialien und ein wärmere und wohnlichere Gestaltung, die hervorragend zur neuen Bedeutung des Bades passt.

Die Materialien müssen beständig und pflegeleicht sein und gleichzeitig auf sinnlicher Ebene überzeugen, also dem Auge schmeicheln und eine angenehme Haptik bieten. Durch die Kombination von kontrastierenden Elementen wird eine Spannung aufgebaut, die das Bad zu einem ganzheitlichen Erlebnis werden lässt. Von der Wandgestaltung bis zum Wasserhahn kann heute das ganz individuelle Wunschbad aus einer Vielfalt von Bausteinen kombiniert werden. Das Ergebnis ist ein Raum, in dem Notwendigkeit und Luxus die engste Verbindung eingehen.

Nicolas Uphaus

Introduction

En partant d'une pièce fonctionnelle dédiée à l'hygiène corporelle, la salle de bains s'est développée en une oasis particulière consacrée à la détente, dans laquelle le corps et l'esprit peuvent tous deux se détendre et se régénérer. Cela se traduit par une conception ingénieuse et réduite, avec l'eau au premier plan, en tant qu'élément prépondérant.

Les formes primitives archaïques et la perfection technologique se complètent parfaitement. La salle de bain moderne n'est plus non plus considérée comme un espace séparé, mais elle se fond avec l'espace nuit. Une combinaison qui prend tout son sens, tant émotionnellement que pratiquement. Les nouveaux matériaux et un aménagement plus chaleureux et plus confortable sont les témoins de cette fusion, qui s'adapte parfaitement à la signification actuelle de la salle de bains.

Les matériaux doivent être durables et d'un entretien facile. Ils doivent présenter, en même temps, une connotation sensorielle favorable, flatter le regard et être agréables au toucher. Cette combinaison d'éléments contrastés créée une énergie qui transforme la salle de bains en un vécu global. Depuis le revêtement mural jusqu'à la robinetterie, la salle de bains de vos rêves combine aujourd'hui une grande diversité d'éléments et s'adapte au goût individuel. En conclusion, c'est un espace qui conjugue intimement la nécessité et le luxe!

Nicolas Uphaus

Introducción

El baño ha pasado de ser un lugar para el aseo corporal a ser un oasis de relajación privado en el que igualmente se pueden relajar y regenerar el cuerpo y el espíritu. Esto se refleja en una decoración simple y estudiada, centrando la atención en el agua como elemento.

Las formas arcaicas básicas y la perfección técnica se fusionan de un modo sublime. Asimismo, el baño moderno ya no se contempla como un espacio aislado, sino vinculado al dormitorio, una combinación que tiene pleno sentido tanto práctico como emocional. De esta fusión nacen nuevos materiales y una decoración cálida y acogedora, que se ajusta de manera extraordinaria con el nuevo concepto de baño.

Los materiales deben ser resistentes y de fácil mantenimiento y a la vez deben agradar a los sentidos, es decir, mimando al ojo y ofreciendo un tacto placentero. Mediante la combinación de elementos que contrastan entre sí, se genera una emoción que constituye una experiencia en sí mismo. Desde los azulejos hasta la grifería, el baño que cada uno desea puede realizarse combinando un amplio abanico de elementos. El resultado es un espacio donde conviven las necesidades básicas y el lujo.

Nicolas Uphaus

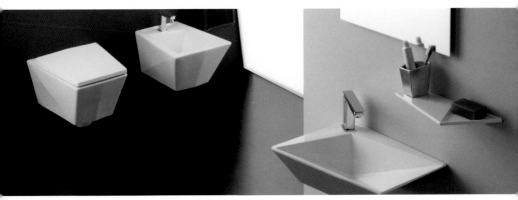

Introduzione

Da semplice spazio destinato alla pulizia del corpo il bagno si è evoluto fino a diventare un'oasi di relax dove corpo e spirito possono ugualmente trovare un momento di pace e rigenerarsi. Questa idea di fondo si rispecchia in una ricerca della forma ridotta e studiata che ponga al centro l'elemento acqua.

Arcaiche forme elementari e perfezione tecnica si completano in modo eccellente. Allo stesso modo, il bagno moderno non è più considerato uno spazio separato, bensì si congiunge con la zona notte – una combinazione che si può apprezzare sia da un punto di vista emozionale sia da un punto di vista pratico. Da questa unione scaturiscono nuovi materiali ed uno stile più caldo ed accogliente che si addice in modo eccellente alla nuova accezione del bagno.

I materiali devono essere durevoli e pratici e nello stesso tempo devono stimolare i sensi, ovvero lusingare la vista ed offrire un piacevole effetto ottico. La combinazione di elementi contrastanti crea una tensione che trasforma il bagno in un'esperienza totalizzante. Dalle pareti al rubinetto, oggi si può organizzare il bagno desiderato da ciascun individuo mettendo insieme una varietà di elementi. Il risultato è uno spazio dove necessità e lusso si sposano in maniera superba.

Nicolas Uphaus

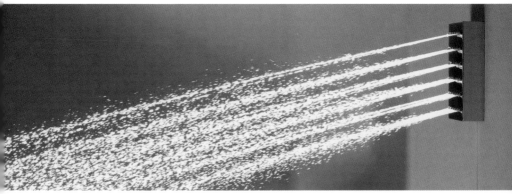

STYLE

The bathrooms on the following pages stage themselves as individual oases of wellness, integrated completely naturally into the rest of the living space. From the washbasin to the shower all elements are naturally combined with the furniture and objects of the living area. A relaxed and very unique atmosphere is created.

Als individuelle, völlig natürlich in den übrigen Wohnraum integrierte Wohlfühloasen inszenieren sich die Bäder auf den nächsten Seiten. Vom Waschbecken bis zur Dusche sind alle Elemente ganz selbstverständlich mit Möbeln und Gegenständen des Wohnbereichs kombiniert. So entsteht eine entspannte und sehr eigenständige Atmosphäre.

Les salles de bains, mises en scène sur les pages suivantes comme des oasis individuelles de bien-être, s'intègrent très naturellement dans le logement. Tous les éléments, du lavabo à la douche, se combinent tout naturellement avec les meubles et les objets de l'espace d'habitation. Il se crée ainsi une atmosphère détendue et personnalisée.

Los baños de las próximas páginas se producen como oasis de bienestar individuales y totalmente naturales, integrados en el resto del hogar. Desde lavabos hasta duchas, todos los elementos están sin duda combinados con los muebles y accesorios del ámbito doméstico. Así se crea una atmósfera relajada e independiente.

Singole oasi del benessere che si integrano in modo del tutto naturale nello spazio abitativo; ecco come si presentano i bagni delle pagine seguenti. Dal lavabo alla doccia, tutti gli elementi si combinano con grande naturalezza con mobili ed oggetti della casa. Per un'atmosfera rilassata e di grande libertà.

Hansgrohe AG / Axor

The following bathrooms are absolutely scaled down in their design without having a clinical effect. This is achieved by the combination of clear shapes and warm, natural colors. The matt surfaces are particularly striking and create a soft, pleasing look.

Die folgenden Bäder sind in ihrer Gestaltung absolut reduziert, ohne nüchtern zu wirken. Erreicht wird dies durch das Zusammenspiel klarer Formen und warmer, natürlicher Farben. Besonders auffällig sind die matten Oberflächen, die eine weiche und angenehme Anmutung erzeugen.

Les salles de bains suivantes proposent un aménagement résolument sobre, sans pourtant paraître dénudé. Cela est rendu possible par la cohérence entre les formes nettes et les coloris chauds et naturels. Les surfaces mates reproduisent une approche douce et agréable et attirent particulièrement l'attention.

Los siguientes baños tienen una decoración totalmente minimalista, sin parecer simple. Esto se consigue mediante la fusión de formas claras y colores cálidos y naturales. Especialmente llamativas son las superficies mates, que producen un suave y agradable encanto.

I bagni sono stati progettati in forma estremamente essenziale, senza però risultare freddi, grazie al gioco combinato di forme semplici e a colori caldi e naturali. In particolare, risaltano molto le superfici opache che creano l'impressione di un ambiente gradevole e delicato.

Boffi

The products in the Scoop range can be described as freestanding bathroom accessories with matt surfaces designed in a clear white on the inside and in vibrant colors on the outside. A column-shaped washbasin forms the heart of the George range, presented on the first double page. Both lines have been designed by Michael Schmidt Design.

Als freistehende Badobjekte können die Produkte der Scoop Serie bezeichnet werden, deren matte Oberflächen innen in klarem Weiß und außen in kräftigen Farben ausgeführt sind. Ein säulenförmiges Waschbecken bildet das Herz der Serie George, die sich auf der ersten Doppelseite präsentiert. Beide Linien wurden von Michael Schmidt Design gestaltet.

Les produits de la collection Scoop peuvent être qualifiés d'objets à installation isolée (non fixés contre une paroi). Leur surface intérieure mate est d'un blanc immaculé et l'extérieur détonne par ses coloris vifs. Un lavabo sur colonne est au cœur de la collection George, présentée sur la première double page. Les deux lignes ont été créées par Michael Schmidt Design.

Como objetos de baño individuales, los productos de la serie Scoop pueden definirse como superficies mates realizadas en blanco claro por dentro y colores fuertes en el exterior. Un lavabo con forma de columna se erige el corazón de la serie George, que figura en la primera página doble. Las dos líneas se han decorado con el diseño de Michael Schmidt.

Complementi da bagno indipendenti: così potremmo definire i prodotti della serie Scoop realizzati con superfici opache, semplicemente bianche nella parte interna ed in tinte forti in quella esterna. Un lavabo a colonna è al centro della serie George che presentiamo nella prima pagina doppia. Le due linee sono state realizzate dallo studio Michael Schmidt Design.

Falper

The following bathroom collection allows a direct fusion of bedroom and bathroom. The soft rectangular design theme defines the look from the mirror to the showerhead. Details and accessories such as the rolling cosmetic container or a matching soap dispenser complete the product range.

Eine direkte Verschmelzung von Schlafzimmer und Bad soll durch die folgende Badserie ermöglicht werden. Das weiche Rechteck als gestalterisches Grundthema bestimmt die Anmutung vom Spiegel bis zum Brausekopf. Details und Accessoires, wie der rollbare Kosmetikcontainer oder ein passender Seifenspender, runden das Programm ab.

Cette collection pour salle de bains doit permettre une fusion directe entre la chambre à coucher et la salle de bains. Le rectangle, thème principal de l'aménagement, détermine l'impression transmise du miroir à la pomme de douche. Les détails et les accessoires, tel le coffre à produits de beauté sur roulette ou le distributeur à savon, complètent la collection.

Mediante la siguiente serie de baños, se posibilita una fusión directa entre dormitorio y baño. El rectángulo suave como tema básico de decoración determina el encanto, desde el espejo hasta la cabeza de la ducha. Los detalles y accesorios, como el contenedor de cosméticos enrollable o un dispensador de jabón adecuado, redondean el programa.

Una serie che consente di combinare insieme ed in modo naturale camera da letto e bagno. Il rettangolo smussato è il motivo figurativo basilare che colpisce a prima vista, a partire dallo specchio e fino alla testa della doccia. Particolari ed accessori, come il portacosmetici girevole o un dispenser per il sapone coordinato, completano il progetto.

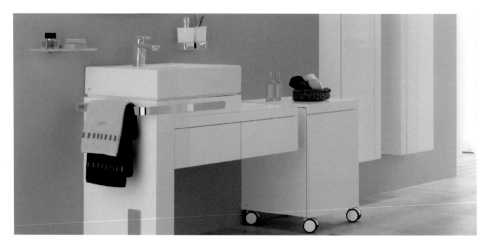

ESPRIT home

The Godmorgon line offers a broad range of materials and colors as well as various models of washbasins, cabinets and mirrors for a free combination. Large cabinets in the washbasins provide storage space and smart details for organization and orderliness inside.

Eine breite Palette an Materialien und Farben sowie verschiedene Modelle an Waschbecken, Schränken und Spiegeln zur freien Kombination bietet die Serie Godmorgon. Große Unterschränke in den Waschtischen sorgen für Stauraum und pfiffige Details für Organisation und Ordnung im Inneren.

La collection Godmorgon propose un large choix de matériaux, de coloris et de modèles divers de lavabos, armoires et miroirs pouvant être combinés librement. Les grands meubles sous-vasques procurent un espace de rangement et de pratiques accessoires facilitent l'organisation intérieure et l'ordre.

La serie Godmorgon ofrece un amplio abanico de materiales y colores, así como diferentes modelos de lavabos, armarios y espejos para combinar libremente. Grandes armarios inferiores bajo el lavabo proporcionan espacio de almacenamiento y vivos detalles para la organización y el orden en el interior.

Un vasto assortimento di materiali e colori, diversi modelli per il lavabo, armadietti e specchi da combinare liberamente; tutto questo è possibile con la serie Godmorgon. Grandi armadietti sotto-lavabo consentono di avere spazio a disposizione e alcuni dettagli intelligenti provvedono ad organizzare e tenere in ordine l'interno.

Ikea

A complete bathroom collection is presented on the following pages—from the bathtub to the tap to the wall tile. Straight, bold lines create large, striking volumes. Black-and-white is used for the surfaces as well as warm brown tones and discreet ornaments.

Auf den folgenden Seiten präsentiert sich ein komplettes Badprogramm – von der Wanne über die Armatur bis zur Wandfliese. Eine gerade, kräftige Linienführung erzeugt große und markante Volumen. Für die Oberflächen kommt schwarz und weiß ebenso zum Einsatz wie warme Brauntöne und dezente Ornamente.

Les pages suivantes présentent une collection complète de salle de bains, depuis la baignoire et la robinetterie jusqu'au carrelage mural. Les lignes droites et vives construisent de grands volumes tranchés. Les surfaces alternent le noir et le blanc avec de chaudes tonalités marron et de discrètes décorations.

En las páginas siguientes se presenta un completo programa de baño, desde la bañera, pasando por la grifería, hasta los azulejos de la pared. Una línea recta y contundente produce un volumen notable y de grandes dimensiones. En las superficies surge tanto el blanco y negro como los tonos marrones y discretos ornamentos.

Protagonista delle pagine seguenti è un programma di bagni completo – dalla vasca alla rubinetteria, alle piastrelle per le pareti. Una linearità retta e decisa crea grandi volumi marcati. Per le superfici sono impiegati il bianco ed il nero così come i toni caldi del marrone e delicati disegni.

JOOP!

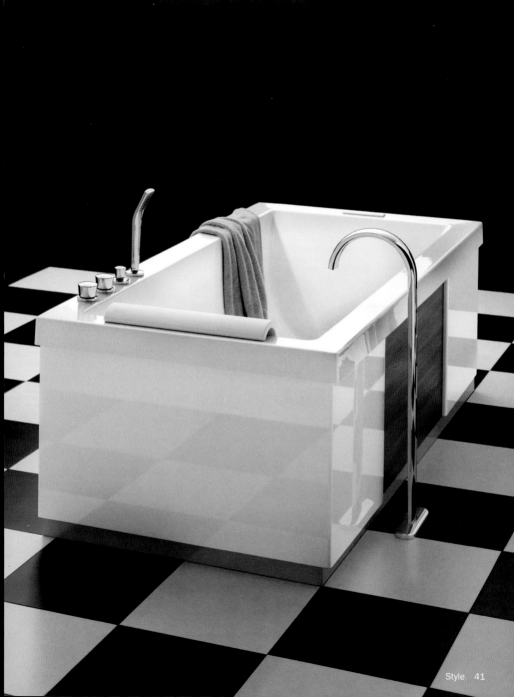

The Starck line 1 (pp. 47–49), designed by Philippe Starck in 1994, has evolved into a modern classic that has brought simple and archaic shapes back into the bathroom. The Starck X line (page 46) on the other hand is very linear and cubic in its design — a real challenge in the production of ceramics.

Die Serie Starck 1 (S. 47–49), von Philippe Starck bereits im Jahr 1994 entworfen, hat sich zu einem modernen Klassiker entwickelt, der schlichte und archaische Formen wieder ins Bad gebracht hat. Die Serie Starck X (S.46) hingegen ist sehr linear und kubisch ausgelegt – eine echte Herausforderung in der Keramikherstellung.

La collection Starck 1 (pp. 47–49), créée par Philippe Starck en 1994, s'est développée en un grand classique et a réintroduit les formes pures et archaïques dans la salle de bains. La collection Starck X (page 46), par contre, est très linéaire et cubique dans ses interprétations. Un véritable défi pour la création de céramiques.

La Serie Starck 1 (pp. 47–49) de Philippe Starck, diseñado ya en el año 1994, se ha convertido en un clásico moderno, que ha devuelto al baño las formas sencillas y arcaicas. La Serie Starck X (pág. 46) por el contrario, se ha concebido de forma muy lineal y cúbica– un auténtico reto en la fabricación de cerámica.

La serie Starck 1 (pp. 47–49), progettata da Philippe Starck già nel 1994, è diventata una moderna opera classica ed ha nuovamente introdotto nel bagno forme semplici ed arcaiche. La serie Starck X (pag. 46), invece, è molto lineare e si presenta in forme cubiche – un'autentica provocazione nella creazione dell'industria ceramica.

Duravit

There are still gold-plated water taps in existence—today, however, they are embedded into an ambience that is able to merge clarity and abundance in one space. These luxury bathrooms combine a classic aura with the selected materials for an overall opulent look.

Es gibt sie noch, die vergoldeten Wasserhähne – heute sind sie allerdings in ein Ambiente eingebettet, das Klarheit und Überfluss in einem Raum vereinen kann. Diese luxuriösen Bäder verbinden eine klassische Ausstrahlung mit ausgewählten Materialien zu einer opulenten Gesamtanmutung.

Les robinets dorés existent toujours encore! Ils se sont cependant intégrés aujourd'hui dans un environnement capable de conjuguer limpidité et opulence dans un unique espace. Ces bains luxueux combinent une projection classique à l'aide de matériaux sélectionnés avec une approche globale d'abondance.

Todavía existen los grifos dorados, que hoy están integrados en un ambiente en el que se puede fusionar claridad y abundancia en un espacio. Estos lujosos baños fusionan un ambiente clásico con selectos materiales, produciendo un rico encanto global.

Esistono ancora i rubinetti placcati d'oro – oggi li troviamo però installati in un ambiente che riesce a conciliare rigore ed esuberanza in un unico spazio. Questi bagni di lusso riescono a raccordare un'influenza classica con materiali selezionati e restituiscono nel complesso un'impressione di magnificenza.

THG Paris

The following pages show the variety of ways the bathroom can be inspired by a living room and linked to it. No sterile bathrooms are created here, but rather comfortable rooms that invite relaxation with new materials, decorations and layouts.

Die folgenden Seiten zeigen, auf welch vielfältige Art und Weise das Bad vom Wohnraum inspiriert sein und mit diesem verbunden werden kann. Nicht sterile Nasszellen werden hier geschaffen, sondern behagliche Räume, die mit neuen Materialien, Dekoren und Layouts zum Entspannen einladen.

Les pages suivantes montrent les multiples manières qu'une salle de bains peut s'inspirer de l'espace d'habitation et lui être uni. Ici, l'on ne conçoit pas des coins toilettes stériles, mais d'agréables espaces qui, grâce à l'utilisation de nouveaux matériaux, décorations et présentations, vous invitent à la détente.

En las páginas siguientes se puede observar las numerosas formas en las que se puede inspirar el baño y estar unido en el espacio en el que transcurre la vida. No se crean estrictamente baños, sino espacios agradables, que invitan al relax mediante nuevos materiales, decoración y diseño.

Le pagine che seguono mostrano come il bagno possa essere ispirato in vario modo dallo spazio abitativo e come riesca ad essere collegato con esso. Qui non si creano locali da bagno asettici, bensì si sviluppano spazi accoglienti che con nuovi materiali, nuove decorazioni e nuovi allestimenti invitano al relax.

Villeroy & Boch

MATERIAL

Ceramic traditionally plays an important role in the bathroom owing to its robustness and value. It is hard to improve on its features. Modern advancements—either through pushing the technical limits or through special surface coatings—emphasise this position.

Das Material Keramik hat durch seine Robustheit und Wertigkeit im Bad traditionell einen hohen Stellenwert. Es ist in seinen Eigenschaften kaum zu ersetzen und moderne Weiterentwicklungen – sei es durch das Ausreizen der formalen Möglichkeiten oder durch spezielle Oberflächenbeschichtungen – unterstreichen diese Position.

La robustesse et la durabilité de la céramique confèrent une importante valeur à la salle de bains traditionnelle. Ses propriétés sont pratiquement irremplaçables et l'amélioration constante dont elle bénéficie, soit en épuisant toutes ses facultés ou en développant des finitions spéciales pour ces surfaces, soulignent cet avantage.

La cerámica tiene tradicionalmente en el baño una gran importancia como material, gracias a su resistencia y valor. Dadas sus características, es difícilmente sustituible y el desarrollo moderno, ya sea mediante el aprovechamiento de las posibilidades formales o revestimientos especiales de superficies, subrayan esta posición.

Tradizionalmente la ceramica nel bagno è un materiale molto importante per la sua resistenza ed il suo pregio. Grazie alle sue qualità è un materiale insostituibile e anche le sue moderne evoluzioni – sia che si tratti della ricerca sulle diverse possibilità di stile sia che si tratti di speciali rivestimenti – confermano questa opinione.

Ceramics

Glass is a very versatile material and most similar to water with its transparency and appearance. Glass bathtubs and showers can present the pure essence of the element as well as creating a special openness and clarity in the design. Glass is naturally essential just as a mirror.

Glas ist ein sehr vielseitig einsetzbares Material und dem Wasser durch seine Transparenz und Anmutung am nächsten. Gläserne Wannen und Duschen können das Element ganz pur präsentieren und schaffen zudem eine besondere Offenheit und Klarheit in der Gestaltung. Ebenfalls unverzichtbar ist Glas natürlich als Spiegel.

Le verre est un matériau à utilisation très polyvalente qui, par sa transparence et son aspect, se rapproche le plus de l'eau. Les baignoires et douches en verre présentent ce matériau d'une façon très pure, donnant, de plus, une vision et une clarté toute particulière à la présentation. Le verre est également irremplaçable en tant que miroir.

El cristal es un material que se puede emplear de muchas formas, cercano al agua en transparencia y encanto. Este elemento se puede presentar en su forma más pura en bañeras y duchas de cristal, proporcionando también una sensación de apertura y claridad al diseño. Asimismo, el cristal es por supuesto irremplazable como espejo.

Il vetro può essere usato in modo molteplice ed è il materiale che si avvicina di più all'acqua per la sua trasparenza e per l'effetto che crea. Vasche e docce di vetro ci restituiscono l'elemento completamente incontaminato nella sua purezza e inoltre combinano una speciale trasparenza e semplicità nella loro forma. Allo stesso modo, non si può naturalmente rinunciare al vetro come specchio.

Glass

HOESCH

Stone is a very original material in the bathroom, used for high quality wall covering or in pebble form as stimulating flooring. Even the production of washbasins or complete washstands is possible. Stone is also ideally suitable to set the tone in the décor of the space.

Ein sehr ursprüngliches Material im Bad ist Stein, eingesetzt zur hochwertigen Wandverkleidung oder in Kieselform als sinnlich stimulierender Bodenbelag. Sogar die Produktion von Waschbecken oder ganzen Waschtischen ist möglich. Stein eignet sich darüber hinaus optimal, um Akzente in der Dekoration des Raumes zu setzen.

La pierre est un matériau utilisé dans la salle de bains depuis l'origine. Elle sert de revêtement de haute qualité pour les parois ou, sous forme de galets, permet de créer un revêtement de sol stimulant les sens. Même la fabrication de lavabos ou de plans vasques est possible. La pierre est idéale, en outre, pour marquer un style dans la décoration de la pièce.

Un material primigenio en el baño es la piedra, empleada como revestimiento de paredes de gran valor o en forma de lajas como simulador para los sentidos del revestimiento del suelo. Incluso es posible producir lavabos o equipo integrados de lavabo completos. La piedra es además óptima para imprimir carácter a la decoración del espacio.

La pietra è un materiale che implica uno stile molto naturale per il bagno, sia quando viene impiegata per pregiati rivestimenti delle pareti, sia quando viene adoperata in ciottoli per un pavimento che sia stimolante per i sensi. La si può impiegare anche per produrre lavabi o interi piani con lavabi. Inoltre la pietra è perfetta per enfatizzare la decorazione dello spazio.

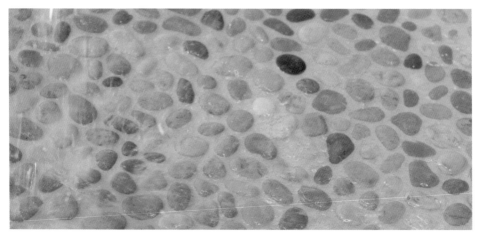

Stone

Wood is a versatile, natural material that represents an excellent contrast to glass and ceramic in the bathroom. Whether as clearly designed bathroom furniture or flooring—the warm brown tones and the individual texture transport value and well-being and complete the overall look of the dream bathroom.

Holz ist ein vielfältiges, natürliches Material, das im Bad einen hervorragenden Kontrast zu Glas und Keramik darstellt. Ob als klar gestaltetes Badmöbel oder als Bodenbelag – die warmen Brauntöne und die individuelle Maserung transportieren Wertigkeit und Wohlgefühl und komplettieren die Gesamt-anmutung des Traumbades.

Le bois est un matériau polyvalent et naturel. Il forme un contraste extraordinaire avec le verre et la céramique. Ses chaudes tonalités marron et les dessins individuels de ses nervures confèrent un sentiment de qualité et de bien-être au mobilier ou au revêtement de sol de la salle de bains, complétant l'image globale de la salle de bains de rêve.

La madera es un material variado y natural, que representa un contraste extraordinario con el cristal y la cerámica. Tanto como mobiliario claro de baño o como recubrimiento del suelo, los cálidos tonos marrones y las vetas individuales imprimen valor y sensación de bienestar y completan el encanto global del baño ideal.

Il legno è un materiale naturale dalle molte varietà e adoperato nel bagno crea un contrasto marcato a confronto con il vetro e con la ceramica. Che si trovi nel semplice arredo del bagno oppure nel rivestimento per il pavimento, in entrambi i casi i caldi toni del marrone e le tipiche venature trasmet-tono un senso di preziosità e di benessere e completano l'impressione generale di un bagno da sogno.

Wood

ELEMENTS

For true relaxation, a bathtub is essential. Generous, freestanding designs are dominant, the style variety ranges from circular to oval or square. Bathtubs are partly enhanced by elaborate coverings, integrated lighting or whirlpool function.

Zur echten Entspannung ist eine Badewanne unverzichtbar. Großzügige, freistehende Ausführungen sind dominierend, die Formvielfalt reicht von kreisrund über oval bis eckig. Teilweise werden die Wannen aufgewertet durch aufwändige Verkleidungen, integrierte Beleuchtung oder Whirlpool-Funktion.

La baignoire est indispensable pour une véritable détente. Les modèles aux dimensions généreuses, prévues pour une implantation isolée, dominent. Les formes sont multiples et vont des rondes et ovales, aux angulaires. Les baignoires se voient en partie revalorisées par des revêtements coûteux, un éclairage intégré ou des fonctions de bain bouillonnant.

Una bañera es fundamental para una verdadera relajación. Predominan las confecciones espléndidas e independientes, la variedad de formas abarca desde círculos u óvalos hasta ángulos. En parte se revalorizan mediante costosos revestimientos, iluminación integrada o función Whirlpool.

Una vasca da bagno è fondamentale per ottenere un autentico relax. Oggi spiccano modelli molto ampi e pezzi unici, la varietà delle forme spazia da quella rotonda a quella ovale o ad angolo. Le vasche hanno in parte riacquistato importanza anche grazie a rivestimenti preziosi, ad impianti di illuminazione integrati o alla funzione di idromassaggio.

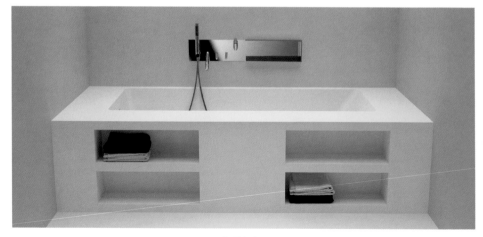

Bathtubs

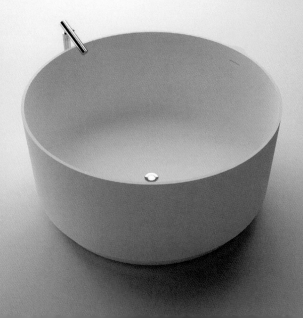

A shower is always refreshing and invigorating. The most beautiful models are presented on the following pages: spacious with extensive glazing and partly as a unifiying element between bedroom and bathroom. Modern showers have developed into a spa in the smallest space with many extra functions.

Eine Dusche ist stets erfrischend und belebend. Die schönsten Modelle präsentieren sich auf den nächsten Seiten: geräumig, mit großflächiger Verglasung und teilweise als verbindendes Element von Schlaf- und Nassbereich. Moderne Duschen haben sich durch viele Zusatzfunktionen zum Spa auf kleinstem Raum entwickelt.

Une douche est toujours rafraîchissante et vivifiante. Les plus beaux modèles font leur présentation sur les pages suivantes : spacieux, avec de grandes surfaces vitrées et servant, partiellement, d'élément de liaison entre les espaces eau et nuit. De nombreuses fonctions complémentaires ont transformé les douches modernes en un spa concentré sur un espace réduit.

Una ducha es siempre refrescante y estimulante. En las páginas siguientes se presentan los modelos más bonitos: espaciosos, con amplio acristalamiento y en parte como elemento de unión entre dormitorio y baño. Las duchas modernas se han convertido gracias a sus múltiples funciones adicionales en Spa en pequeños espacios.

Una doccia è sempre rinfrescante e stimolante. Nelle pagine seguenti proponiamo i modelli più belli: spaziose, con vetrate molto ampie, a volte veri e propri elementi di raccordo tra il vano letto e il vano bagno. Grazie a molte funzioni supplementari, le docce moderne si sono evolute in Spa in miniatura.

Showers

The variations in washbasins are extremely diverse. The theme of the integrated, classic washbasin is still used in the most diverse variations. In addition there are cubic, completely freestanding variants and also increasing are variants, so that a model can be found to suit every personal taste.

Die gestalterischen Variationen zum Waschbecken sind äußerst vielfältig. Das Thema der aufgesetzten, klassischen Waschschüssel wird nach wie vor in verschiedensten Formen bedient. Darüber hinaus gibt es kubische, komplett freistehende und verstärkt auch asymmetrische Varianten, so dass für jeden persönlichen Geschmack ein passendes Modell zu finden ist.

Il existe de très nombreuses variations dans les modèles proposés de lavabos. Le thème classique des cuvettes posées se décline, comme par le passé, en différentes variantes. Il existe, de plus, des variantes cubiques à montage complètement isolé complétant les modèles asymétriques, de telle sorte que chacun trouvera un modèle à son goût.

Las variaciones creativas de los lavabos son extremadamente amplias. El tema del lavabo clásico incorporado se sirve todavía en diferentes variantes. Además hay cúbicos, totalmente independientes y se refuerzan también las variantes asimétricas, de modo que hay un modelo adecuado para cada gusto.

Le variazioni stilistiche dei lavabi sono quanto mai molteplici. Il tema del catino classico viene proposto come sempre nelle più diverse variazioni. In più si trovano versioni a cubo, allestimenti in pezzi completamente a sé stanti e sono largamente diffusi anche i modelli asimmetrici; insomma, non si può non trovare un modello adatto per ogni gusto.

Sinks

The toilet and bidet are veering away from the well-known oval form. Current models are marked by diverse experiments in form, particularly in cube formats. An especially unusual product that is connected to the past can be seen on pages 138-147.

WC und Bidet entfernen sich formal zur Zeit von der bekannten ovalen Form. Vielfältige Formexperimente, insbesondere kubische Formate, kennzeichnen die aktuellen Modelle. Ein besonders ausgefallenes Produkt, das an vergangene Zeiten anknüpft, findet sich auf den Seiten 138-147.

Les vécés et les bidets s'éloignent actuellement de la forme traditionnelle. Diverses expérimentations sur les formes, particulièrement les modèles cubiques, caractérisent les propositions actuelles. Un modèle particulièrement insolite, renouant avec les temps passés, vous est présenté sur les pages 138 à 147.

El inodoro y el bidet se alejan hoy en día de la conocida forma ovalada. Los modelos actuales se caracterizan por la variedad de experimentos realizados con las formas, en particular formatos cúbicos. En las páginas 138 a 147 figura un producto especialmente extraño, referido al pasado.

Oggi WC e bidet si discostano dalla consueta forma ovale. Diversi esperimenti sulla forma, soprattutto su quella cubica, caratterizzano i modelli attuali. Nelle paginas 138-147 si trova una creazione particolarmente insolita che si ricollega al passato.

Lavatories

The times of simple taps and shower knobs are long gone. Sophisticated design with constantly new surprises and exclusive details should inspire the user. Useful add-on elements such as an integrated shower on the washstand extend the range of functions.

Die Zeiten einfacher Wasserhähne und Duschgarnituren sind längst vorbei. Ausgefeilte Gestaltung mit immer neuen Überraschungen und exklusiven Details soll den Benutzer begeistern. Nützliche Zusatzelemente, etwa eine integrierte Brause am Waschtisch, erweitern den Funktionsumfang.

L'époque des simples robinets et robinetteries de douche est révolue depuis longtemps. Des systèmes sophistiqués proposent toujours de nouvelles surprises et des détails exclusifs censés convaincre l'utilisateur. Des éléments complémentaires pratiques comme, par exemple, une pomme de douche intégrée au lavabo, élargissent les champs des fonctionnalités proposées.

Ya han pasado los tiempos de griferías y accesorios de ducha sencillos. El usuario debe entusiasmarse con cuidados diseños que incorporan constantemente nuevas sorpresas y detalles exclusivos. Las funciones se ven ampliadas gracias a útiles elementos adicionales, como una ducha integrada en el lavabo.

Ormai non si può pensare più di avere semplici rubinetti e accessori per la doccia. Forme perfezionate con sempre nuove sorprese e dettagli esclusivi devono coinvolgere il consumatore in un entusiastico interesse. Alcuni accessori utili, come la doccetta integrata nel lavabo, ampliano la gamma delle funzioni proposte.

Mountings

Elements

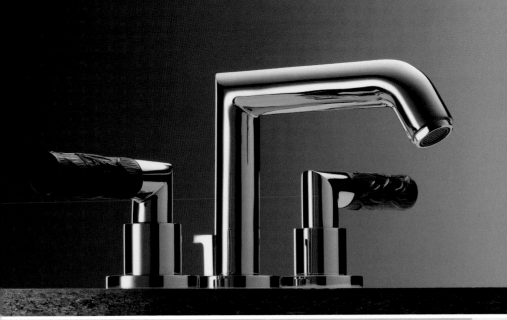

Simple white tiles? Long since have other moisture-resistant and easy-care alternatives prevailed, in synthetic resin, natural stone or plastic. Naturally tiles are still used, but refined in their design and finish, in special formats as well as combined with other materials.

Einfach weiße Fliesen? Längst haben sich auch andere feuchtigkeitsresistente und pflegeleichte Alternativen durchgesetzt, sei es Kunstharz, Naturstein oder Kunststoff. Natürlich kommen immer noch Fliesen zum Einsatz, aber dann raffiniert gestaltet und veredelt, in besonderen Formaten sowie mit anderen Materialien kombiniert.

Simplement des carreaux blancs? Des modèles alternatifs, faciles d'entretien et résistants à l'humidité, en résine synthétique, pierre naturelle ou encore en matière plastique, se sont imposés depuis longtemps sur le marché. Les carreaux continus, bien entendu, à être utilisés. Leur finition a cependant été améliorée et les modèles proposés sont devenus plus élégants, les formes sont plus variées ou combinant avec d'autres matériaux.

¿Simplemente azulejos blancos? Hace tiempo que se imponen también otras alternativas resistentes a la humedad y fáciles de mantener, ya sea resina sintética, piedra natural o plástico. Claro que todavía se emplean azulejos, pero más acabados y refinados, en especial los formatos, combinados también con otros materiales.

Semplici piastrelle bianche? Ormai da tempo si sono diffuse ed affermate anche soluzioni alternative come la resina sintetica, la pietra viva o la materia plastica, anch'esse resistenti all'umidità e di semplice manutenzione. Naturalmente, le piastrelle non sono state completamente dimenticate, ma si trovano oggi in forme più raffinate e più pregiate, in formati particolari o combinate con altri materiali.

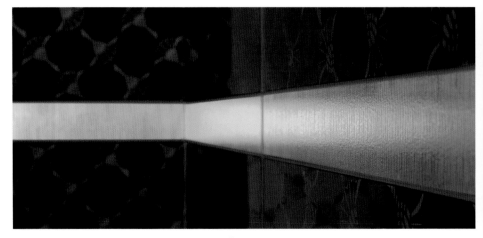

Wall Covering

Even in the bathroom there are many little details that make the final finish. Mirrors, shelves, hand towel rails, and thought-out details in bathroom furniture, or decoration, such as vases and candles, turn a bathroom into a space of real relaxation. Not to be ignored, also the right lighting.

Auch im Bad sind es die vielen Kleinigkeiten, die die Sache erst rund machen. Spiegel, Ablagen, Handtuchhalter und durchdachte Details der Badmöbel, oder Dekoration wie Vasen und Kerzen machen ein Bad zum Raum echter Entspannung. Nicht zu vernachlässigen ist auch die passende Beleuchtung.

Dans la salle de bains également, les nombreux accessoires améliorent sensiblement l'ensemble ! Les miroirs, les étagères, les porte-serviettes et les ingénieux détails des meubles de bain ou encore la décoration, composée de vases et de bougies, transforment votre salle de bains en un espace privilégié pour la détente. Un éclairage adéquat est un autre élément qui ne doit pas être négligé.

A la adecuada decoración del baño contribuyen muchas pequeñas cosas. Espejo, bandejas, colgadores de toallas y estudiados detalles del mobiliario del baño, o decoración con jarrones y velas, hacen del baño un espacio consagrado a una auténtica relajación; un elemento fundamental es la iluminación apropiada.

Anche nel bagno si possono trovare diversi piccoli oggetti che contribuiscono a rendere l'ambiente armonioso. Specchi, armadietti, portasciugamani e dettagli d'arredo studiati attentamente, oppure elementi decorativi quali vasi e candele rendono il bagno lo spazio giusto per un autentico relax. Da non trascurare, infine, anche un adeguato sistema di illuminazione.

Accessories

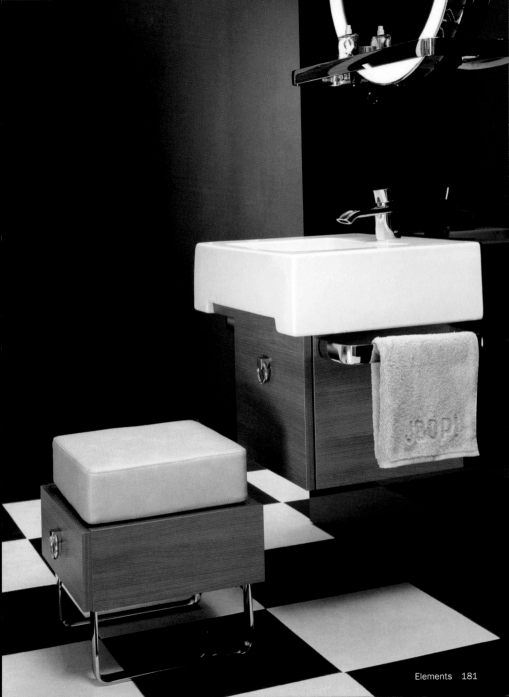

CUSTOM MADE

by INTACT-BAD

This bathroom was integrated into the architecture of a villa from the 1920s with its simple and spacious appearance. Oak floorboards and black granite blocks form a pleasant contrast to the round and soft bathroom accessories and there is a direct access to the bedroom "sleeping area".

Dieses Bad wurde in seiner schlichten und großzügigen Anmutung in die Architektur einer Villa aus den 1920er Jahren integriert. Eichendielen und schwarze Granitblöcke bilden einen angenehmen Kontrast zu den runden und weichen Sanitärobjekten und es besteht ein direkter Übergang zum Schlafbereich.

Cette salle de bains, simple et généreuse dans son apparence, a été intégrée dans une villa datant des années 1920. Des boiseries en chêne et des blocs de granit noir forment un agréable contraste avec les appareils sanitaires aux formes rondes et douces, créant une transition directe avec l'espace nuit.

Este baño, con su sutil y generoso encanto, se integró en la arquitectura de una villa de los años 1920. Vestíbulos de roble y bloques negros de granito constituyen un contraste agradable con los sanitarios redondeados y suaves y tiene un acceso directo a la zona del dormitorio.

Con il suo colpo d'occhio semplice e straordinario, questo bagno è stato inserito nell'architettura di una villa degli anni 1920. Listelli di quercia e blocchi di granito nero formano un piacevole contrasto con gli elementi dei sanitari dalla morbida forma rotonda e nell'insieme restituiscono un'idea di apertura e di continuità con il vano notte.

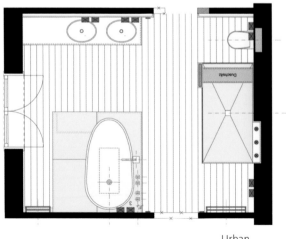

Urban

The sweeping view over Düsseldorf is a special feature in both of the following bathrooms in the same apartment. The first bathroom adjoins the bedroom directly in terms of space and design. The second is designed as a separate wellness oasis with integrated sauna.

Der weite Blick über Düsseldorf ist ein besonderer Vorzug der folgenden beiden Bäder, die zur selben Wohnung gehören. Das erste Bad schließt räumlich und gestalterisch direkt an den Schlafbereich an. Das Zweite ist als separate Wellness-Oase mit integrierter Sauna konzipiert.

La vue panoramique sur Düsseldorf est un privilège tout particulier des deux salles de bains suivantes, appartenant au même logement. La première salle de bains est directement contiguë à l'espace nuit, tant par sa situation que par son aménagement. La deuxième, intégrant un sauna, a été conçue comme une oasis différenciée de bien-être.

La amplia panorámica sobre Düsseldorf es una ventaja particular de los dos baños siguientes, que se encuentran en el mismo piso. El primer baño está unido espacial y decorativamente con el dormitorio. El segundo está concebido como un oasis de Spa con sauna integrada.

Un'ampia veduta su Düsseldorf è il pregio particolare di questi due bagni che si trovano nello stesso appartamento. Sia dal punto di vista dello spazio che dell'arredo, il primo bagno risulta immediatamente inserito nel vano notte. Il secondo, invece, separato e con sauna integrata, è stato ideato come un'oasi di benessere.

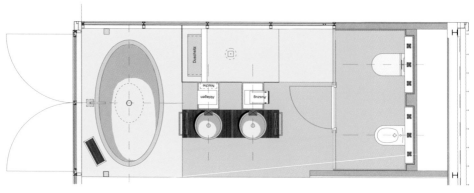

Bathroom With a View

The dream of a private wellness spa has been turned into reality in this space. A spacious bathtub with whirlpool function and a shower stall with integrated sauna invite relaxation. The clear black-and-white appearance and cleverly thought-out mood lighting form a convincing unit.

Der Traum einer privaten Wellness-Anlage wurde in diesem Raum verwirklicht. Eine großzügige Wanne mit Whirlpoolfunktion und eine Duschkabine mit integriertem Dampfbad laden zum Entspannen ein. Die klare schwarz-weiße Optik und ausgeklügeltes Stimmungslicht bilden eine überzeugende Einheit.

Disposer d'une installation privée de bien-être est un rêve qui s'est vu réalisé dans cet espace. Une baignoire aux formes généreuses, incluant un système de bain bouillonnant ainsi qu'une cabine de douche avec bain de vapeur intégré, vous invite à la détente. La présentation lumineuse, dans les coloris noirs et blancs ainsi qu'un éclairage d'ambiance sophistiqué, complète cette unité particulièrement réussie.

En este espacio se hace realidad el sueño de contar con unas instalaciones privadas de Spa. Una generosa bañera con función Whirlpool y una cabina de ducha con baño de vapor integrado invitan a relajarse. La clara óptica en blanco y negro y una planificada luz de ambiente conforman una rotunda unidad.

In questo spazio, il sogno di una struttura privata per il benessere è diventato realtà. Una splendida vasca con funzione idromassaggio ed una cabina per la doccia con bagno turco integrato possono solo invogliare al relax. Il semplice effetto ottico del bianco e nero ed una sofisticata illuminazione per una giusta atmosfera danno forma ad un insieme convincente.

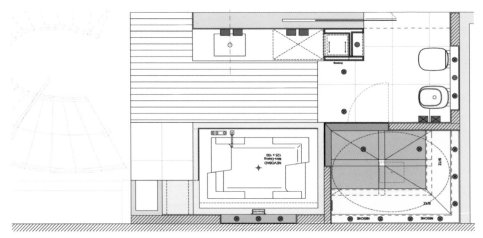

Home Spa

nice steam
a bath

Brilliant white marble slabs and marble plaster are crucial in defining the appearance of this bathroom, offering a spacious shower and a lavish whirlpool bath. The lighting system is particularly worth mentioning. The right mood is set with a starry sky directly over the bath and a matching color LED module.

Strahlend weiße Marmorplatten und Marmorputz bestimmen maßgeblich die Anmutung dieses Bades, das mit einer geräumigen Dusche und einer aufwändigen Whirlpool-Wanne aufwartet. Hervorzuheben ist das Lichtsystem: Ein Sternenhimmel direkt über der Wanne sowie ein farblich anpassbares LED-Modul sorgen für die richtige Stimmung.

Des plaques et enduit de marbre blanc lumineux marquent la présentation de cette salle de bains, complétée par une douche spacieuse et une baignoire aux généreuses dimensions, équipée d'un bain bouillonnant. Le système lumineux est particulièrement ingénieux : un ciel étoilé, directement situé au-dessus de la baignoire, ainsi que des diodes électroluminescentes à variation de couleurs, assure l'atmosphère idéale.

Losas y revoques de reluciente mármol blanco determinan nítidamente el encanto de este baño, que cuenta con una amplia ducha y una selecta bañera Whirlpool. Cabe destacar el sistema de iluminación: tanto un cielo de estrellas sobre la bañera, como un módulo LED en el color apropiado proporcionan el ambiente correcto.

Lastre di marmo bianco lucido e guarnizioni in marmo determinano in modo deciso il colpo d'occhio di questo bagno arredato con un'ampia doccia ed una ricca vasca con idromassaggio. Non si può non notare il sistema di illuminazione: un cielo stellato direttamente sulla vasca ed un modulo a LED che si può adattare cromaticamente restituiscono la giusta atmosfera.

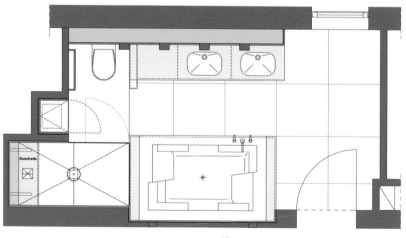

Lit up

Crystal is the design theme of this luxury bathroom and is reflected in all the details: from the fronts of the bathroom furniture to the glittering lighting to the crystal glass handles of the fittings. Luxury is emphasised with a spacious bath and two shower stalls, one of which is fitted with a sauna.

Der Kristall ist das Gestaltungsthema dieses luxuriösen Bades und zeigt sich in allen Details: von den Fronten der Badmöbel über die glitzernde Beleuchtung bis hin zu den Kristallglasgriffen der Armaturen. Eine großzügige Wanne und zwei Duschkabinen, von denen eine mit einem Dampfbad ausgestattet ist, unterstreichen den luxuriösen Anspruch.

Le cristal, thème central de l'aménagement de cette somptueuse salle de bains, est présent dans tous les détails : depuis les façades des meubles de bain et l'éclairage étincelant jusqu'aux poignées en verre de la robinetterie. Une baignoire aux dimensions généreuses et deux cabines de douche, l'une d'entre elle équipée d'un bain vapeur, souligne la finition luxueuse.

El cristal es el tema decorativo de este lujoso baño, presente en todos los detalles: desde los frontales del mobiliario del baño sobre y la brillante iluminación hasta los mangos de cristal de los mandos. Una amplia bañera y dos cabinas de ducha, una de ellas equipada con un baño de vapor, realzan estas lujosas exigencias.

Il cristallo è il motivo formale di questo bagno di lusso e si mette in mostra in tutti i dettagli: dagli elementi frontali dei mobili del bagno all'illuminazione scintillante fino alle manopole dei rubinetti in cristallo. Una splendida vasca e due cabine per la doccia – una delle quali con bagno turco integrato – mettono in evidenza il desiderio di lusso.

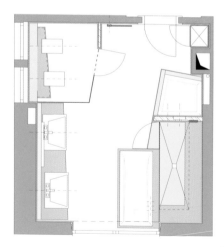

Glamorous

In this bathroom the washing, showering and bathing areas have been arranged as separate units, with the shower stall playing a special role as a central cube. Nice details such as a built-in flush mirror cabinet over the washstand or separately controlled light elements round off the composition.

Bei diesem Bad wurden die Bereiche Waschen, Duschen und Baden in separaten Einheiten angeordnet, wobei die Duschkabine als zentraler Kubus eine besondere Position einnimmt. Schöne Details, wie der flächenbündig eingelassene Spiegelschrank über dem Waschtisch oder separat ansteuerbaren Lichtelemente, runden die Komposition ab.

Dans cette salle de bains, les espaces lavabo, douche et bain sont présentés en unités séparées et la cabine de douche, cube central, occupe une position privilégiée. Des détails soignés, comme cette armoire encastrée à miroirs, à pose affleurée et située au-dessus du lavabo ou encore des éléments lumineux à commande séparée, complètent la composition.

En este baño, los ámbitos de lavabo, ducha y baño están organizados en unidades independientes, en el que la cabina de ducha ocupa una posición especial como cubo central. Bonitos detalles, como el armario con espejo encastrado a ras de la superficie sobre el lavabo o elementos de iluminación que se pueden dirigir independientemente, redondean la composición.

In questo bagno le zone del lavabo, della doccia e della vasca sono organizzate in unità distinte e la cabina doccia assume una posizione particolare, essendo un cubo posto nel centro. Completano la composizione alcuni dettagli molto eleganti, come l'armadietto a specchio che si trova sopra il lavabo, incassato e a filo con le pareti, o gli elementi per l'illuminazione orientabili separatamente.

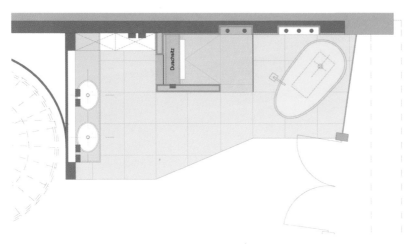

Natural Stones

Even under a pitched roof, in a former children's room, a convincing bathroom can be installed. A raised floor was necessary for the supply lines and this opens up the room at the same time. The spacious shower stall offers room for two people and the skylight gives a direct view into the sky while bathing.

Auch unter einer Dachschräge, im ehemaligen Kinderzimmer, lässt sich ein überzeugendes Bad einrichten. Für Versorgungsleitungen war ein Zwischenboden nötig, der den Raum jedoch gleichzeitig auflockert. Die großzügige Duschkabine bietet Platz für zwei Personen und das Dachfenster während des Bades einen direkten Blick in den Himmel.

Même sous le plafond incliné de cette ancienne chambre d'enfant, une jolie salle de bains trouve sa place! La pose des circuits d'alimentation a demandé l'installation d'un faux plancher qui apporte maintenant un élément d'ambiance supplémentaire. La cabine de douche, de généreuses dimensions, offre un espace suffisant pour deux personnes et la lucarne s'ouvre sur une vue du ciel.

También bajo un techo inclinado, en la que era la habitación de los niños, puede confeccionarse un excelente baño. Ha sido necesario un suelo intermedio para las conducciones, aligerando el espacio al mismo tiempo. La generosa cabina de ducha proporciona espacio para dos personas y la ventana del techo, con el que el baño cuenta con una vista directa al cielo.

Anche sotto un tetto spiovente, in una mansarda precedentemente adibita a camera per bambini, si può allestire un bagno più che credibile. Per le condutture delle varie forniture è stato creato un doppio pavimento grazie al quale, tuttavia, lo spazio risulta alleggerito. La splendida cabina doccia può ospitare due persone e la finestra-lucernaio consente una vista verso il cielo mentre si sta facendo il bagno.

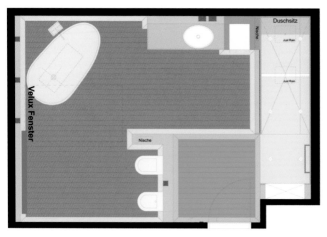

Elegant Simplicity

This spacious bathroom has been designed completely in sandstone from the washstand to the shower cubicle. The warm and friendly color tones of the natural materials give a completely pure effect with the clear blocks. The retangular design theme is taken up again in the atmospheric lighting.

Dieses großzügige Bad wurde vom Waschtisch bis zur Duschkabine komplett in Sandstein ausgeführt. Der warme und freundliche Farbton des Naturmaterials kommt durch die verwendeten klaren Quader ganz pur zur Geltung. Das Rechteck als Gestaltungsthema wird in der stimmungsvollen Beleuchtung wieder aufgegriffen.

Cette grande salle de bains a été entièrement réalisée en grès, depuis le lavabo jusqu'à la cabine de douche. La chaude tonalité accueillante de ce matériau naturel est rehaussée par la limpidité des blocs de pierre de taille utilisés. Le rectangle, thème central de l'aménagement, est repris par un éclairage évocateur de l'ambiance.

Este espléndido baño se ha confeccionado en arenisca desde el lavabo hasta la cabina de la ducha. El tono cálido y agradable de los materiales naturales se impone a través de la clara sillería de piedra empleada. El rectángulo como tema decorativo se vuelve a captar en la agradable iluminación.

Questo straordinario bagno è stato realizzato completamente in pietra arenaria, dal lavabo fino alla cabina doccia. La tonalità di colore calda e piacevole di questo materiale naturale viene messa in risalto nella sua purezza dai conci chiari utilizzati. Il rettangolo, motivo formale del bagno, torna anche nel suggestivo sistema di illuminazione.

Sandstone

INDEX

AF NEW YORK
22 West 21st Street, 5th Floor
New York, NY 10010
USA
Phone: +1 / 212 / 243 54
Fax: +1 / 212 / 243 24 03
info@afnewyork.com
www.afnewyork.com

Agape srl
Via Po Barna 69
46031 Correggio Micheli di Bagnolo
San Vito-Mantova
Italy
Phone: +39 / 0376 / 25 03 11
Fax: +39 / 0376 / 25 03 30
info@agapedesign.it
www.agapedesign.it

Antrax IT srl
Via Boscalto 40
31023 Resana TV
Italy
Phone: +39 / 0423 / 71 74
Fax: +39 / 0423 / 71 74 74
antrax@antrax.it
www.antrax.it

ArtQuitect
Dolors Graners, 79 Cardedeu
Barcelona
Spain
Phone: +34 / 93 / 844 40 70
Fax: +34 / 93 / 844 40 71
artquitect@artquitect.net
www.artquitect.net

Boffi S.p.A.
Via Oberdan, 70
20030 Lentate sul Seveso (Milan)
Italy
Phone: +39 / 0362 /53 41
Fax: +39 / 0362 / 56 50 77
info@boffi.com
www.boffi.com

Cesana SpA
Via Dalmazia, 3
20059 Vimercate (Milan)
Italy
Phone: +39 / 039 / 63 53 81
Fax: +39 / 039 / 685 11 66
info@cesana.it
www.cesana.it

Duravit AG
Werderstraße 36
78132 Hornberg
Germany
Phone: +49 / 7833 / 700
Fax: +49 / 7833 / 702 89
info@duravit.de
www.duravit.de

**Esprit home bath concept über
Kludi GmbH & Co. KG**
Postfach 2560
58685 Menden
Germany
Phone: +49 / 2373 / 90 40
Fax: +49 / 2373 / 90 43 33
esprit@kludi.com
www.esprit.com/bath-concept

Falper Srl
Via Veneto, 7/9
40064 Ozzano dell'Emilia BO
Italy
Phone: +39 / 051 / 79 93 19
Fax: +39 / 051 / 79 64 95
info@falper.it
www.falper.it

Franz Kaldewei GmbH & Co. KG
Beckumer Straße 33-35
59229 Ahlen
Germany
Phone: +49 / 2382 / 78 50
Fax: +49 / 2382 / 78 52 00
info@kaldewei.de
www.kaldewei.com

GUNNI & TRENTINO
Castello, 43
28001 Madrid
Phone: +34 / 902 / 15 23 97
Fax: +34 / 91 / 642 44 12
castello@gth.es
www.gunnitrentino.es

Hansgrohe AG
Auestraße 5-9
77761 Schiltach
Germany
Phone: +49 / 7836 / 510
Fax: +49 / 7836 / 51 13 00
info@hansgrohe.com
www.hansgrohe.com

HOESCH Design GmbH
Postfach 10 04 24
52304 Düren
Germany
Phone: +49 / 2422 / 540
Fax: +49 / 2422 / 545 40
info@hoesch.de
www.hoesch-design.com

IKEA Deutschland
Am Wandersmann 2 - 4
65719 Hofheim-Wallau
Germany
Phone: +49 / 180 / 535 34 35
Fax: +49 / 180 / 535 34 36
www.ikea.de

INTACT-BAD GmbH
Grünstraße 15, im stilwerk
40212 Düsseldorf
Germany
Phone: +49 / 211 / 86 22 86 66
Fax: +49 / 211 / 86 22 86 77
info@intact-bad.de
www.intact-bad.de

JOOP! LIVING
Heilwigstraße 33
20249 Hamburg
Germany
Phone: +49 / 40 / 48 09 25 60
Fax: +49 / 40 / 48 09 25 69
customerservice@joop-living.com
www.joop.com

Keramag AG
Kreuzerkamp 11
40878 Ratingen
Germany
Phone: +49 / 2102 / 91 60
Fax: +49 / 2102 / 91 62 45
info@keramag.de
www.keramag.com

Koralle Sanitärprodukte GmbH
Hollwieser Straße 45
32602 Vlotho
Germany
Phone: +49 / 05733 / 140
Fax: +49 / 05733 / 142 95
info@koralle.de
www.koralle.com

Olympia Ceramica srl
Zona Ind.le Loc. Pantalone, 35
01030 Corchiano (VT)
Italy
Phone: +39 / 0761 / 57 33 92
Fax: +39 / 0761 / 57 33 93
info@olympiaceramica.it
www.olympiaceramica.it

ORAS GmbH & Co. KG
Postfach 2103
58634 Iserlohn
Germany
Phone: +49 / 2371 / 948 00
Fax: +49 / 2371 / 94 80 23
info.germany@oras.com
www.oras.com

THG Paris
Gutleutstraße 96
60329 Frankfurt am Main
Germany
Phone: +49 / 69 / 25 78 14 33
Fax: +49 / 69 / 25 78 14 35
info@thg-deutschland.de
www.thg-deutschland.de

Villeroy & Boch AG
Postfach 1120
66688 Mettlach
Germany
Phone: +49 / 6864 / 810
Fax: +49 / 6864 / 81 14 84
information@villeroy-boch.com
www.villeroy-boch.com

Other titles by teNeues

ISBN 978-3-8327-9323-4

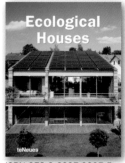

ISBN 978-3-8327-9227-5

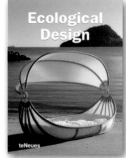

ISBN 978-3-8327-9229-9

ISBN 978-3-8327-9228-2

ISBN 978-3-8327-9307-4

ISBN 978-3-8327-9380-7

ISBN 978-3-8327-9338-8

Interior Pages **Kitchen Design**

Size: **15 x 19 cm**, 6 x 7 ½ in., 224 pp., **Flexicover**, c. 250 color photographs,
Text: English / German / French / Spanish
www.teneues.com